CONTENT

MACHUPICCHU   116

PRESENTING PERU
&
MACHUPICCHU

INTRODUCTION

Peru is a unique and wonderful country which owns an exuberant biodiversity and is the scene of an extraordinary culture. Thus, visiting it is an exceptional and unforgettable experience which awakens one's curiosity and interest to get to know it better, so as to understand it. Therefore, motivated by our visitors' fascination, I decided to undertake a study of different information sources and above all, of texts written by serious researchers who are contributing, from their perspective, in our getting to know, interpret, give value and comprehend the complexity of our natural and cultural heritage. In that way, the book you are starting to read, has as its final purpose, the exposition of Peru's present reality, its geography, history and most visited tourist attractions, and above all, Machupicchu, through a practical tool with easy reading content that provides you the most important data and information.

Indeed, whoever steps on Peruvian soil and journeys across this country, will want to have references on present day Peru and its people, by means of a simple and synthesized information source. Today's Peru is essentially the product of the mixture of two cultures: The Andean and Occidental which, with the passing of time, managed to produce fusions and gave rise to populations with particular ways of life, which still preserve their personality, with values and traits different to those of the rest of the world. The data extracted from official sources, reflect its people's way of thinking and living, as they show a panoramic and general vision which allows us to state that, in spite of its complexity, it is a country which, with much genius, progresses towards its so longed for prosperity. Furthermore, this is why the reader will find in this work, many Quechua names and words, in the aim of transmitting and valuing the Andean culture still alive in our country, and especially, in Cusco. Thus, words or names like "Inka" or "Inkan" are written with "k" instead of "c", because modern Quechua spelling rules have established it that way. Therefore, the first part contains an information summary which gives an insight on present day Peru and the direction in which it is progressing.

Meanwhile, in the second part, you will notice that Peru is a country with an extraordinary natural beauty. Its geography is astonishing, as it shows the coexistence of greatly contrasting sceneries. Likewise, this land of great ecological diversity, shelters and ensures life's continuity, through the multiple and exuberant variety of its flora and fauna. Without a doubt, it is a prized and prodigious space, because of its biological mega-diversity and genetic resources. But, at the same time, it is complex and hostile, due to the drastic climatic changes and violent phenomena which reaffirm that it is far from being a homogeneous country, and therefore, this, in itself, makes it difficult for its inhabitants to adapt to its environment and get integrated in it.

The third part is a quick review of the Andean people's past, since its arrival, more than 15,000 years ago. Emphasis is placed on the Inkan period, for being a summary of the trajectory of the Andean inhabitants and product of the relations that existed between them and their environment. At that time, the Andeans deployed their maximum effort and a great creativity, on the basis of real knowledge and detailed study of geographical features in their surroundings, to intelligently and rationally take advantage of the resources they offered them. Therefore, general welfare was quite normal, as neither hunger nor poverty were known.

As a testimony of what has been said above, Peru is a privileged country, given the richness and variety of its natural and cultural patrimony which makes it very attractive for visitors. Here, nature lovers will be able to enjoy the unimaginable contrasts between beaches, deserts, mountains, valleys, jungle, etc. This is the world in which the Andean people built their history, through a long and deep adaptation process, with the understanding, acceptation, love and full respect of their surroundings, to manage a harmonious cohabitation, and a sample of this is shown through the numerous archaeological remains and a triumphantly living culture. Thus, the fourth part is a compilation of the most visited tourist attractions in Peru, although it is worth saying there is much more to see and enjoy, in a context in which that great common denominator which is the Peruvian people's creativity, is combined with their capacity of adapting to their environment, across the whole Peruvian territory.

I wanted to conclude this work, presenting our most important attraction; Machupicchu, Humanity's Cultural and Natural Patrimony, declared as one of the Seven Wonders of the Modern World. Indeed visiting the Andean civilization's maximum cultural expression, is a dream come true. This is why, in these pages, I wanted to capture a synthesis of the magic that surrounds that eternal city; magic which, for me, remains alive through every single visit, because, although I have seen it more than a thousand times, its spell and magnificence will always be present in my mind. Definitely, Machupicchu is the most important legacy the Inkas left for the whole world.

This book offers an updated, clear and precise vision of the features that define Peru, and I hope it will become a reference tool. My intention is that this guide might be useful to you, as you come with the wish to discover Peru's particularities, as well as its people, the context in which it is developing, its past and some samples of its tourist patrimony. "Presenting Peru and Machupicchu" responds to your need to understand this attractive country which, by itself, incites inquiries and fascinates the most exigent of visitors.

Saydí M. Negrón Romero

PERU IN THE WORLD

The Republic of Peru is an Andean State situated in the Central and Occidental parts of South America, from 0° 01′ 48″ to 18° 21′ 05″ South and between 68° 39′ 27″ and 81° 19′ 34.5″ West.

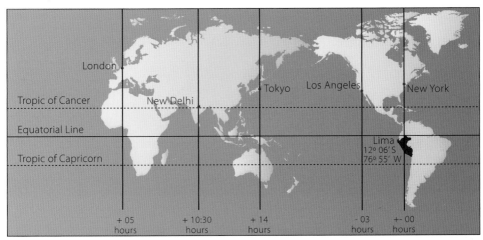

Its extension is of 1,285,216 km². Therefore, this makes it the third country in South America (7.2%), the sixth on the American continent and the twentieth in size, in the world.

Geographical surface comparative frame		
Peru is:		
5.3	times larger than (the)	United Kingdom 243,610 km²
3.4		Japan 377,915 km²
3.6		Germany 357,022 km²
2.5		Spain 505,370 km²
2		France 643,427 km²
2.2	times smaller than (the)	Argentina 2,780,400 km²
6		Australia 7,741,220 km²
6.6		Brazil 8,514,877 km²
7.6		USA 9,826,675 km²
7.8		Canada 9,984,670 km²

TODAY'S PERU

Kind of Government: Democratic Republic.

The Republic of Peru's Constitutional President is democratically elected in the General Political Elections, for a five year term.

In Peru, voting is personal, free, equal, secret and mandatory, up to 70 years of age. (It is optional after that age).

Political Division:

24 departments and one constitutional province, El Callao.

Each department or region is composed of provinces and there are 181 provinces in total.

Each province is composed of districts and there are 1,747 districts in total.

Date of Independence:
July 28, 1821

Capital City: Lima

Currency:
It is the Nuevo Sol (New Sun) which is divided among 100 centimes and circulates in bills and coins.

National Flag and Shield

- Peru's capital city
- Regional capital cities

American Dollars and Euros are accepted in the majority of tourism related businesses, according to the day's exchange rate.

Population

In accordance with the last 2007 census, Peru's population is ascending to 28,220,764 inhabitants.

Population by gender

49.7%   50.3%

Men   Women

By law, majority is reached at 18.

Population according to age groups

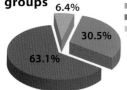

6.4%

30.5%

63.1%

- From 0 to 14
- From 15 to 64
- 65 and over

In 2007, there were 25,923 Peruvians over 95 years of age.

The fecundity rate is of 2.6 children per woman

Population density in Peru

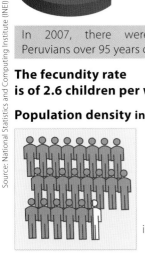

21.3 inhabitants/km²

Population according to the geographical region

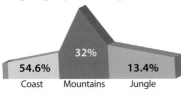

54.6%   32%   13.4%

Coast   Mountains   Jungle

Variation of the population in Peru		
Year	Population	Reference
1532	14 millions	Estimated population*
1548	8,285,000	The Colony's 1st census
1570	2,800,000	Estimated population
1791-1795	1,076,122	The Colony's last census during Peru's Vice-Royalty
1836	1,873,736	1st census of the Republican Period
1876	2,699,105	The 19th century's last census
1940	7,023,110	The 20th century's 1st census
1993	22,661,690	The 20th century's last census
2007	28,220,764	The 21th century's 1st census
2011	29,797,694	Projection of Peru's population
2015	31,151,643	Projection of Peru's population

*Personal appreciation

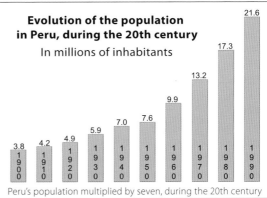

Evolution of the population in Peru, during the 20th century
In millions of inhabitants

21.6

17.3

13.2

9.9

7.6

7.0

5.9

4.9

4.2

3.8

1900 1910 1920 1930 1940 1950 1960 1970 1980 1990

Peru's population multiplied by seven, during the 20th century

The coast is the territory's narrowest region (10.64%) with little water resources. However, this is where the largest cities have developed, sheltering the greater quantity of population.

The jungle is the territory's largest region (57.85%) with great water resources. But, in turn, it is the country's most uninhabited region.

Source: National Statistics and Computing Institute (INEI)

Population's evolution according to the geographical region

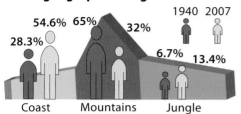

	1940	2007
Coast	28.3%	54.6% / 65% ... 32%
Mountains		
Jungle	6.7%	13.4%

Distribution of the population per area

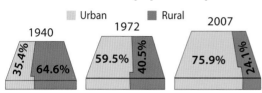

Urban / Rural

1940 — 35.4% / 64.6%
1972 — 59.5% / 40.5%
2007 — 75.9% / 24.1%

Source: INEI

Among some factors which facilitated the migration process from the mountains and jungle to the coast, and from the countryside to the city, are considered:

- The country's centralist tendency which turned the capital city (Lima) into the main axis of the majority of activities.
- The Agrarian Reform established by Juan Velasco Alvarado's Military Government, in 1969.
- Terrorist violence, between 1980 and 1992.
- The coast's growth, due to the "export boom" that started in the decade of the 90's.

Immigration to Peru, from the time of the conquest, to the beginning of the 20th century		
Spain / Africa		480 years ago
Arriving from	Europe	England Italy Germany Austria France	19th century and beginning of 20th century
	Asia	China Japan Korea	
	Among others	Arabs Jews etc.	

Flores Galindo sustains that "during the first thirty years of colonization, on today's Peruvian territory, there were between 4,000 and 6,000 Europeans, of whom a little over 500 were non Spanish", and among them, he mentions Portuguese, Mediterraneans (Italy and Mediterranean islands), Germans, British, French and others still.

With the passing of time and events, a great mixture has taken place, which already allows us to clearly distinguish among the indigenous and mixed race, without mentioning the people of European, African or Asian ascendance (Mainly Chinese and Japanese).

Most populated cities	2007	2011	2015
1 Metropolitan Lima & Callao	8,472,935	9,303,788	9,904,727
2 Arequipa	749,291	925,667	969,284
3 Trujillo	682,834	899,709	957,010
4 Chiclayo	524,442	829,051	857,405
5 Piura	377,496	724,230	764,968
6 Iquitos	370,962	545,095	563,249
7 Cusco	348,935	420,030	450,095
Lima constitutes 30.58% of Peru's total population			

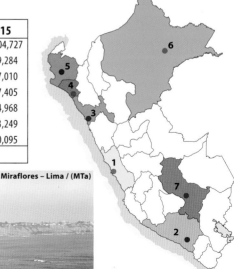

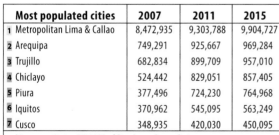

Miraflores – Lima / (MTa)

Life expectancy

Life expectancy at birth has increased in a considerable way during the last years, given the improvement of healthcare. In addition, vital indicators that ensure health (Drinkable water, sewer system, electrification and sanitary infrastructure) are being modernized, Peru's child mortality rate is in constant decrease, the level of education is ever improving, and above all, income levels are slowly increasing.

Life expectancy at birth	2005 - 2010	73.1 years	Source: INEI - Peru

		76 years		Source: Health and Education Social Indicators for Latin America, published by the WHO (World Health Organization) - 2009
Life expectancy at birth	2009	Women 77 years	Men 75 years	
Healthy life expectancy at birth	2009	66.5 years		
		Women 67 years	Men 66 years	

Education

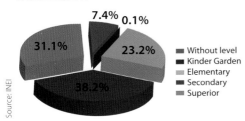

Source: INEI

- 7.4%
- 0.1%
- 31.1%
- 23.2%
- 38.2%

- ■ Without level
- ■ Kinder Garden
- ▦ Elementary
- ■ Secondary
- ▦ Superior

Basic and regular education is mandatory and free in public schools, for initial, primary and secondary levels.

Superior Education Institutes offer 3 year study programs.

University Education requires a minimum of 5 years of study.

(Non university students: 15.1% / University students: 16%)

Levels of education	Initial		Primary			Secondary		
Cycles	I	II	III	IV	V	VI	VII	
Age	0-2	3-5*	6	7	8	9	10	11	12	13	14	15	16
Grades	nursery	kinder garden	1°	2°	3°	4°	5°	6°	1°	2°	3°	4°	5°
Minimum yearly study hours	900 hours		1,100 hours			1,200 hours		

Source: Ministry of Education

*Only this last year is mandatory, in order to start primary education.

Private educational institutions develop more hours than those foreseen in the standards.

Official language

Spanish, along with native languages.

Peru is one of the countries with the greatest ethno-linguistic and cultural diversity, on the American continent.

I. P. Escot, in her book "Multi-linguism in Peru", proposes 19 linguistic families and 43 Andean and Amazonian languages.

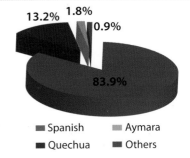

- 13.2%
- 1.8%
- 0.9%
- 83.9%

- ■ Spanish
- ▦ Aymara
- ■ Quechua
- ■ Others

Procession of the Lord of Miracles

Pilgrimage of the Lord of Qoyllur Rit'i

Carnival allegory

Religion

The religion that predominates and identifies Peru is the Christian faith and especially, the Catholic Church which gives its origin to a popular Catholic religion; product of its fusion (Syncretism) with the Andean religion, around which many festivities are celebrated.

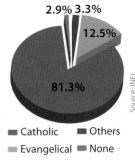

2.9% 3.3%
12.5%
81.3%

Source: INEI

■ Catholic   ■ Others
■ Evangelical ■ None

Peru has nearly three thousand popular, local, traditional and religious holydays, as well as recently created or assimilated holydays which take place in different parts of the territory, with a diversity of hues. But, the festivity that is celebrated as much on the coast, in the mountains and jungle, as in the city and countryside, is that of Carnival, manifesting itself with a particular touch in each place.

Official calendar of non workable holidays		
Month	Day or date	Celebration
January	1st	New Year
February or March	Variable Sunday	Carnival *
March or April	Holy Thursday Holy Friday Easter Sunday	Easter Week
May	1st 2nd Sunday	Labor Day Mother's Day
June	3rd Sunday 24th	Father's Day Farmer's Day Saint John Baptist Inti Raymi or Sun's Feast *
	29th	Saint Peter and Saint Paul's Day
July	28th 29th	Independence Day and National Festivities
August	30th	Saint Rose of Lima's Day
October	8th	Battle of Angamos
November	1st	All Saints' Day
December	8th 25th	Immaculate Conception's Day Christmas

* Are not considered as official holydays.

Generally, the celebration of Carnival is a festivity in which converge ritual, gratitude, love, beauty, play, joy, music, dancing, mischievousness, some satire, irony, humor, color, pranks, eating and drinking.

Economy

During the last 20 years, Peru's economy has registered a constant growth, as it stood out as one which grew most in Latin America. In spite of the fact that, in 2009, it was affected by the world financial crisis, with a growth of only 0.9%, in 2010, a greater increase was achieved, that reached 8.8%.

This economic growth makes it so that the quality of life of Peruvian society, is improving. But, there are still sectors of the population, which are not being attended by the State.

During the past years, the main sources of growth of Peru's economy are the mining industry, agro-industry and tourism.

Tourism

The country's major attraction is Machupicchu. All tourists who visit it pass through the city of Cusco; reason for which the following frame is a good reference, due respect to the number of visitors Peru receives yearly.

Evolution of tourist arrivals in the Province of Cusco, classified by departure points									
Order	Country	Years							
		Rank	2007	Rank	2008	Rank	2009	Rank	2010
1	United States of America	1	145,700	1	178,691	1	263,121	1	138,148
2	Other European Countries	2	66,030	2	77,832	3	97,673	2	61,417
3	Great Britain	3	51,704	3	57,218	2	167,471	4	42,102
4	France	4	39,655	4	46,320	4	61,709	3	45,997
5	Germany	5	29,442	6	30,876	6	43,079	9	26,319
6	Spain	6	27,856	7	30,639	5	47,690	10	24,186
7	Japan	7	27,744	5	31,709	11	26,733	11	17,542
8	Argentina	8	26,272	8	30,290	7	35,212	5	37,555
9	Canada	9	24,593	10	28,551	9	27,786	8	28,014
10	Oceania (Australia, etc.)	10	23,132	9	28,685	10	27,390	7	28,762
11	Brazil	11	18,775	11	23,609	8	34,809	6	30,996
12	Italy	12	16,839	12	17,349	12	14,326	12	13,791
13	Mexico	13	9,836	15	10,670	15	8,947	14	11,307
14	Colombia	14	8,436	14	11,748	14	12,632	13	12,312
15	Chile	15	8,152	13	15,445	13	14,254	15	11,242
16	Israel	16	7,055	16	7,575	16	8,112	16	6,598
18	Other American countries	17	6,704	19	3,867	18	4,996	19	3,970
18	Other Asian countries	18	4,962	17	5,603	21	4,051	17	4,911
19	Venezuela	19	3,924	18	5,171	17	5,224	18	4,179
20	Ecuador	20	3,640	22	3,098	20	4,391	21	3,283
21	Central America	21	3,076	20	3,397	19	4,765	20	3,545
22	North Korea	22	2,056	26	2,142	28	1,301	29	1,371
23	Africa	23	2,001	29	1,931	26	1,973	25	2,157
24	Uruguay	24	1,953	21	3,111	22	3,507	27	2,092
25	China	25	1,901	27	2,067	25	2,147	22	2,675
26	Bolivia	26	1,864	25	2,207	24	2,266	24	2,432
27	South Korea	27	1,482	23	2,744	23	2,916	26	2,008
28	India	28	1,190	24	2,289	27	1,895	23	2,500
29	Paraguay	29	1,160	29	1,318		0	28	1,782
30	Taiwan / Singapore	30	856	30	755		0	30	1,130
TOTAL			567,990		666,907		930,376		574,323

Exports

The diverse economic policies, in relation with foreign trade, have contributed to the growth of traditional and non-traditional exports, emphasizing the promotion of exports with added value.

Main export products:

Fish flour, fish oil, cotton, sugar, coffee, copper, tin, iron, gold, refined silver, lead, zinc, molybdenum, crude oil and by-products (INEI).

In addition:

Alpaca fiber (Wool), anchovies, artichokes, asparagus, avocadoes, bananas, bees' honey, butterflies, camu camu (*Myrciaria dubia*), cat's claw (*Uncaria tormentosa*), ceramics, cereals, cochineal, chillies and spices, chocolates, flowers, giant corn of Cusco and purple maize, guinea pigs, grapes, handicraft, jewels, lemons, lúcuma, maca (*Lepidium meyenii*), mangos, natural gas, olives, onions, oranges, oregano, pisco, prawn, potatoes, quinoa (*Chenopodium quinoa*), sacha inchi (*Plukenetia volúbilis*), sea algae, (Step) horses, shoes, tangelos, tangerines, tara (*Caesalpinia spinosa*), textiles, trout, turkeys, wines, wood, yacon (*Smallanthus sonchifolius*), etc., (ADEX).

SOME AGRO-EXPORT PRODUCTS PRESENT IN OVER 140 COUNTRIES

Chillies · Corn · Camu camu · Asparagus · Artichokes · Sacha inchi · Cacao · Coffee · Onions · Mango · Banana

Peru is first in organic coffee export trade.

Imports

Main import products:

Crude oil from petroleum, technology (Machinery and transportation equipments, mobile phones, photo cameras, televisions, etc.), pharmaceutical products, chemical fertilizers, polypropylene, hard yellow corn, raw soy oil and wheat (INEI).

A UNIQUE COUNTRY

Due to its geographical situation and singular factors, Peru presents a great variety of regions, with a ground relief that encompasses almost the totality of all known geographical accidents: From the sea shelf, passing by the coast and the Andes' heights, all the way to the Amazon. These features create ecosystems with great variety of natural resources, which makes it that Peru is considered as one of the world's few mega-diverse countries.

Peru's climates

Peru is fully contained within the Southern Tropical Zone and so, its climate should be hot, rainy and humid. However, the conjunction of several elements and factors determines the variation and diversity of conditions and kinds of climates and weather.

Geographical Latitude

Its proximity with the Equatorial Line makes it that the Sun's rays reach it in a more direct way, during the whole year, thus determining the duration of the day and hours of sunlight, with little variations between seasons.

Being close to the Equatorial Line ensures an intense solar radiation which has influence on the quality of agricultural and livestock products.

Peru's climates	
Factors	**Elements**
Latitude Altitude (Andean Cordillera) Humbolt Sea Current Equatorial or El Niño Sea Current	**Winds:** - South Pacific Anticyclone - Equatorial Cyclone - South Atlantic Ocean's Anticyclone **Rainfalls / Temperature / Pressure / Humidity**

Sun rays: The same quantity of light and energy illuminates more surface and produces a moderate temperature.

Sun rays: The same quantity of light and energy illuminates more surface and produces a higher temperature.

■ **The Equatorial Current or El Niño**
It is a hot water current which provokes rains on the North coast and exerts a permanent influence on the Peruvian Sea, elevating the general temperature on the coast and Northern mountain ranges. (When the El Niño Current moves more towards the South, this produces the El Niño Phenomenon).

■ **South Pacific Ocean's Anticyclone**
Air masses that contain high atmospheric humidity which, as they get colder, due to the Humboldt Current's influence, form a ceiling of persistent low clouds, without any ascending movement, nor turbulences, from May to October, which makes it so that the quantity of solar radiation decreases.

■ **The Cordillera of the Andes**

■ **Humbolt Current or Peruvian Oceanic Current**
Cold waters accompanied by the South Pacific Ocean's Anticyclone, both motivating atmospheric stability which does not favor condensation and inhibits rainfall. It is responsible for the coastal desert and dryness of the Andes' Occidental mountain range.

■ **Equatorial Cyclone**
Masses of humid and hot air that provoke rainfalls on the Amazonian region, as they collide with the Andes.

■ **South Atlantic Ocean's Anticyclone**

17

Altitude

It is a factor determined by the Cordillera of the Andes which runs from South to North and acts as a barrier, blocking the passing of West-bound winds coming from the Atlantic Ocean, which condensate and precipitate on its Oriental flank.

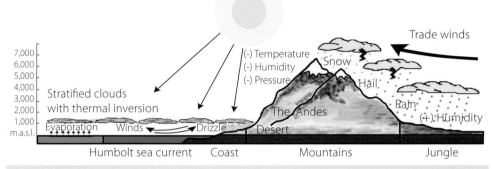

The Pacific Coast in Peru is the world's only dry tropic, with a stable climate and natural greenhouse conditions.

THE CORDILLERA OF THE ANDES

It was born as a consequence of successive phases of tectonic uplifting and folding generated by the superposition of the Nazca and South American plates, about 80 million years ago. These were alternated with violent volcanic episodes and later on, with the glaciations of the Quaternary Era, which deeply eroded the previous orography and marked the present relief.

The Cordillera of the Andes is the only mountainous system in the country. Its influence is decisive on the relief, climate and water resources, as well as on the different vertical levels, etc., creating many differentiated and unequal vital spaces which greatly contribute to its diversity.

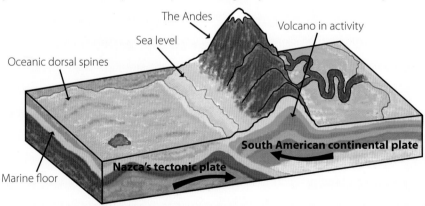

The Nazca plate is submerged in the mantle. The subduction area makes it that it is highly prone to earthquakes and volcanic activity.

The Cordillera of the Andes reaches 7,240 km. in length and runs through Argentina, Chile, Bolivia, Peru, Ecuador, Colombia and Venezuela.

Mount Huascaran in Ancash

Mount Chopicalqui in Ancash

Huascaran and the Seven Summits			
1	Everest	8,848 m.s.n.m.	Asia and the world
2	Aconcagua	6,959 m.s.n.m.	South America
	Huascaran	6,768 m.s.n.m.	Peru
3	Mount McKinley	6,194 m.s.n.m.	North America
4	Kilimanjaro	5,895 m.s.n.m.	Africa
5	Elbrus	5,633 m.s.n.m.	Europe
6	Vinson Massif	5,140 m.s.n.m.	Antarctica
7	Puncank Jaya	5,030 m.s.n.m.	Oceania

Peru possesses 18 mountain ranges and 3,044 glaciers, which amounts to being one of the world's 20 largest glacier areas.

Peru's lowest point is the depression of Bayovar, in Piura, which is 37 meters under sea level and the highest is Mount Huascaran, in Ancash, with 6,768 m.a.s.l. and is the highest in the world's tropical area.

The snow-capped mountains and glaciers are found above 5,000 m.a.s.l.

The White Cordillera is 180 km. long, with 722 glaciers, for which it is considered as the planet's largest tropical glacier mountain range.

The snow-capped Ausangate is the highest in the Vilcanota Cordillera, and it can be observed from the city of Cusco on a clear day.

Peru's seven highest mountains		
Snow-capped peak	Altitude	Mountain range
Huascaran	6,768 m.s.n.m.	White
Yerupajá	6,632 m.s.n.m.	Huayhuash
Coropuna	6,425 m.s.n.m.	Ampato
Chopicalqui	6,400 m.s.n.m.	White
Huautsan	6,395 m.s.n.m.	White
Ausangate	6,384 m.s.n.m.	Vilcanota
Tunsho	6,369 m.s.n.m.	White

Mount Ausangate in Cusco

Mount Chimboya in Puno

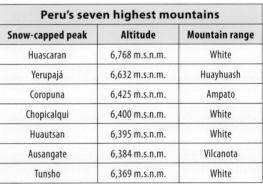

Rainfalls and Temperature

In Peru, the behavior of temperatures and rainfalls changes substantially, between one region and another, as well as from one period of the year to another.

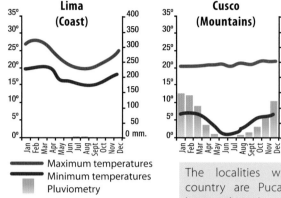

- ─── Maximum temperatures
- ─── Minimum temperatures
- ▨ Pluviometry

Source: National Weather Forecast and Hydrology Service (SENAMHI)

The localities with extreme temperatures in the country are Pucallpa – Ucayali, reaching 42°C and Imata – Arequipa, with -25° C.

Hydrology

Peru contains great quantities of soft water which is unequally distributed. There are glaciers, rivers, lakes, lagoons and underground waters, to which can be added a considerable annual rainfall.

AMAZON RIVER

During the 20th century, the Nile River was considered as the "Longest River in the World". However, the last research reveal that the most powerful, widest, deepest and longest river on the planet, is the Amazon River, with a course of 6,800 km.; that is, 105 km. longer than the Nile.

Rivers

Peru possesses a great variety and quantity of rivers, among which stands the Ucayali, as one of the main tributaries of the Amazon.

Almost 50 rivers reach the Pacific Ocean and most of them have seasonal patterns.

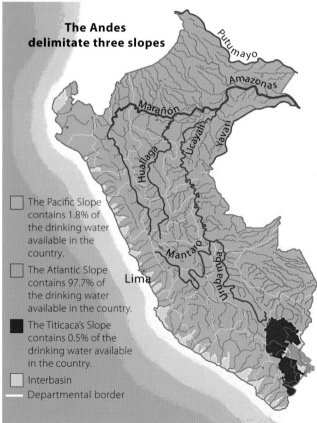

The Andes delimitate three slopes

☐ The Pacific Slope contains 1.8% of the drinking water available in the country.

☐ The Atlantic Slope contains 97.7% of the drinking water available in the country.

■ The Titicaca's Slope contains 0.5% of the drinking water available in the country.

☐ Interbasin

── Departmental border

The Titicaca Slope is endorheic and occupies the Collao High Plateau.

Ramis River on the High Plateau (MTa)

River in Huaraz

Largest Rivers in Peru

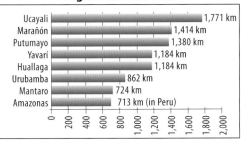

Ucayali	1,771 km
Marañón	1,414 km
Putumayo	1,380 km
Yavarí	1,184 km
Huallaga	1,184 km
Urubamba	862 km
Mantaro	724 km
Amazonas	713 km (in Peru)

Amazon River

(MS)

Lakes and Lagoons

Officially, there are 12,201 lakes and lagoons with different characteristics, and the majority of them are found above 4,000 m.a.s.l.

Largest Lakes in Peru

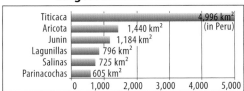

Titicaca	4,996 km² (in Peru)
Aricota	1,440 km²
Junín	1,184 km²
Lagunillas	796 km²
Salinas	725 km²
Parinacochas	605 km²

El Dorado Lagoon at dusk

(A/P)

The Titicaca and the world's largest lakes

Peru & Bolivia	Africa	North America	Europe & Asia
Titicaca 8,562 km²	Victoria 68,422 km²	Superior 82,100 km²	Caspian Sea 371,000 km²

Umayo Lagoon on the High Plateau

Dawn on Lake Titicaca

(GB)

(CV)

(AR)

PERU, A COUNTRY OF GREAT DIVERSITY

Due to the mega-biodiversity it presents, Peru is considered by biologists as the "Noah's Ark of Modern Times".

Diversity of Ecosystems

Thanks to climatic elements and factors, such as the great heterogeneity of the physical relief, determined by the Cordillera of the Andes flanked by the Pacific Ocean and Amazonian Basin, Peru enjoys the presence of the majority of the planet's ecological systems which shelter thousands of species of flora and fauna, along with other natural resources, to which are added geological formations presenting the most varied landscapes and production areas.

Describing Peru's natural patrimony and understanding the interrelations among the environment's diverse factors, is a very difficult mission to fulfill. However, thanks to the appraisable work of researchers, the following can be mentioned:

1.- Traditionally, Peru is divided into three natural regions that run longitudinally. This is a proposal of Hispanic origin which, due to its simplicity, is insufficient to explain the diversity of ecosystems.

Jungle

Pacific Ocean

Mountains

Coast

Coast	10.6%
Mountains	31.8%
Jungle	57.6%

22

2.- In 1946, Pulgar Vidal formulated, with scientific criteria, a division in eight natural regions, based on the location of ecosystems, in accordance with altitude. That classification is known and managed since pre-Hispanic time.

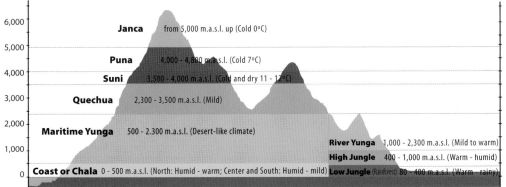

Janca from 5,000 m.a.s.l. up (Cold 0°C)

Puna 4,000 - 4,800 m.a.s.l. (Cold 7°C)

Suni 3,500 - 4,000 m.a.s.l. (Cold and dry 11 - 12°C)

Quechua 2,300 - 3,500 m.a.s.l. (Mild)

Maritime Yunga 500 - 2.300 m.a.s.l. (Desert-like climate)

River Yunga 1,000 - 2,300 m.a.s.l. (Mild to warm)

High Jungle 400 - 1,000 m.a.s.l. (Warm - humid)

Coast or Chala 0 - 500 m.a.s.l. (North: Humid - warm; Center and South: Humid - mild)

Low Jungle (Rainforest) 80 - 400 m.a.s.l. (Warm - rainy)

The Puya de Raymondi is a plant which grows in the puna (Highlands), over 4,000 meters above sea level. It grows over 10 m. in height, reaches 3 m. in diameter in 100 years, and dies off after having produced thousands of flowers.

(MTa)
(LG)
(AS)
(MTa)

3.- Later on, Brack Egg established a classification in eleven eco-regions, as the result of an integration of physical features and ecological factors that allow recognizing in more detail, Peru's ecological diversity.

1 Cold sea of the Peruvian Current: Highly productive.

2 Tropical sea: It gives a unique character to the coast and sea, in the North of Peru.

3 Desert and coastal hills: From 0 to 1,000 m.a.s.l. These are semi-hot and very dry.

4 Equatorial dry forest: From 0 to 1,500 m.a.s.l.. It is tropical, hot and dry, with high temperatures. In the Marañón River Basin, it nearly reaches 2,800 m.a.s.l.

5 The Pacific tropical forest: Upon rare occasions, it drops to less than 500 m.a.s.l. It is humid, with high temperatures.

6 Mountainous steppes: From 1,000 to 3,800 m.a.s.l. They offer two kinds of climates: The mild sub-humid and cold climate.

7 The high plains (Puna) and High Andes: The puna is cold and runs from 3,500 / 3,800 to 5,200 m.a.s.l. The High Andes, with permanent snow and freezing climate, run from 5,200 to 6,768 m.a.s.l.

8 The moor (Wide barren plains): It is located North of the Porculla Mountain Pass (2,145 m.a.s.l.), that region's lowest point, and is going up above 3,200 / 3,500 m.a.s.l. It offers special climatic conditions, but, generally, its climate is humid.

9 High jungle forests: From 500 / 800 to 2,500 m.a.s.l. They offer two types of climates: The semi-hot and humid, between 800 and 2,500 m.a.s.l., with rainfalls over 2,000 mm. / year and the cold one, between 2,500 and 3,800 m.a.s.l., with rainfalls of about 700 mm. / year.

10 The Amazonian tropical forest or lower jungle: It goes up to 800 m.a.s.l. and is tropical hot.

11 The palm tree savannah: 400 m.a.s.l., is hot, humid and tropical.

NATURAL AND BIOLOGICAL DIVERSITY OF PERU'S ECOSYSTEMS

The variety of climates, different natural regions and combinations of eco-regions allow a broad natural, biological and production diversity.

- Out of the 117 life zones recognized in the world, 84 exist in Peru.
- Out of the 32 types of climates existing on Earth, 28 are found in Peru.
- It is the sixteenth country with the greatest quantity of soft water.
- Out of the total of tropical jungles that exist in the world, Peru possesses 13% of them.
- The territory's diversity of habitats determines the existence and distribution of an immense diversity of flora and fauna, among which we find many endemic species.
- There are nearly 4,400 native plant species of known use.
- The Earth's deepest canyons are located in Peru: Cotahuasi, with 3,535 meters and Colca, with 3,400 meters.
- The third highest Cataract in the world is Gocta with 771 meters.
- The longest waves in the world; Las Izquierdas (The Lefters) (to surf), can be found on Malabrigo Beach, in La Libertad.
- The highest sand dune in the world is Cerro Blanco, in Ica, with 2,078 m.a.s.l.
- The mightiest, largest, widest and deepest river with the most extended basin in the world; The Amazon, has its origin on Peruvian territory.
- Peru possesses 60% of the world's highest navigable lake, the Titicaca.
- The Peruvian Sea is one of the seven richest seas in marine fish. In addition, it possesses the world's most important diversity and biomass of hydro-biological resources (1st producer of fish flour in the world).
- The greatest concentration of marine birds can be observed on the Guaneras Islands.
- Peru is the world's 3rd country in mining wealth and reserves (1st gold, lead, zinc, silver and tellurium producer in Latin America. It is 1st silver and 5th gold producer in the world).
- In Trujillo (Peru), there are the remains of the world's largest mud brick built city; Chan Chan, with a surface of 20 km².
- Peru is the cradle of potatoes and the first country with the greatest diversity of shapes, colors,

Meat kebabs

Tamales

Guinea pig

Peru is considered as the country with the most varied gastronomy in the world, according to the Guiness Book (It offers over 491 dishes).

Stuffed hot pepper

Purple corn chicha

Quinua soup

A la huancaina potato

(Mm)

Pumpkin cream

Pisco sour

Fish ceviche

(Mm)

The Peruvian cocktail known as "Pisco Sour" is elaborated with pisco, lemon, egg, sugar and ice.

Pisco is obtained through the fermentation and distillation of grape juice.

Sauteed spaghetti

Chicken juane

Grilled trout

Pork crackling

Grilled chicken

Purple corn jello and Rice pudding

Picarones

Historical Sanctuary of Machupicchu   Taquile Island on Lake Titicaca

LIST OF WORLD HERITAGE SITES IN PERU		Since
Natural Patrimony	• Huascaran National Park • Manu National Park	1985 1987
Mixed Patrimony	• Historical Sanctuary of Machupicchu • Rio Abiseo National Park	1983 1990
Non-material Cultural Patrimony	• Oral Patrimony and Cultural Manifestations of the village of Zápara (Shared with Ecuador) • Textile Art from Taquile • Two Andean dances: The Cisors' Dance and the Huaconada de Mito	2008 2008 2010
Cultural Patrimony	• City of Cusco • Archaeological Site of Chavin de Huantar • Chan Chan's Archaeological Zone • Historical Center of Lima • Lines and Geoglyphs of Nazca and Pampas de Jumaná • Historical Center of Arequipa • Sacred City of Caral - Supe	1983 1985 1986 1988 1994 2000 2009

The Cisors' Dance   Mountaineering in the White Cordillera

SOME SPECIES OF THE PERUVIAN FAUNA

Class	Birds	Fish	Primates	Mammals	Amphibians	Reptiles	Butterflies
Nr. of species	1,827	1,800-855	35	462	411	387	Thousands
World ranking	1st	1st	2nd	3rd	3rd		1st
% of the world's total	20%	10%					

Our own elaboration based on the information of the Ministery of Environment.

Butterflies
"More than 1,300 species, in the locality of Pakitza, Manu". (1)

Source: www.peruecologico.com.pe/opciones.html (1), (2), (3)

There are, millions of species of molluscs, arachnids and insects
"About 5,000 species of insects were found on a single tree in Tambopata, Madre de Dios, of which 80% were new to science". (2)

Flamingo
Fam. Phoenicopteridae

Inkan necklace hummingbird
Coeligena (inka) torquata

Ara ararauna
Macaw

Pterocnemia pennata
Suri

1,827 species of birds
"On one km² of jungle in Madre de Dios, one can see up to 800 species of birds". (3)

Rupicola peruviana
(TI) Cock of the rocks

Sarcoramphus papa
Royal condor

▲ The Suri lives in high Andean areas, and is the largest non-flying bird in Peru. One of these birds' most interesting features, is that the male is a great father, as it incubates the eggs during 40 days, and then, it raises, feeds and protects its offspring. Unfortunately, it is in danger of extinction.

The Little Cock of the Rocks or Tunqui is Peru's National Bird. ▲ It presents a sexual dimorphism which makes it so that the male displays a beautiful plumage and its mating dance is a genial spectacle.

Penelope albipennis
White winged turkey

1,800 species of marine fish and 855 continental fish.

The Paiche is one of the largest soft water fish in the world, and it lives in rivers and still lakes (Cochas) of the Amazonian Basin. It can reach 3 meters in length and weighs about 250 kilos. Its meat is delicate and very much appreciated.

Fam. Ardeidae
White heron

The carachi is one of the few native species that remain in Lake Titicaca. ▼

Carachi
Orestias spp

Arapaima gigas

(MV) Anchovies
Fam. Engraulidae

Leopardus pardalis
Ocelot

Andean fox
Dasycion culpaeus

(AB)
Otaria flavescens Sea wolf or seal

Mazama americana
Colored deer

462 species of mammals

Tremarctos ornatus
Spectacled bear

Puma concolor
Puma

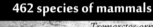

Tayassu tajacu
Wild hog

Dasyprocta fuliginosa
Añuje

Nasua nasua
Ringed-tail coati
Bald uakari

35 species of primates

The Amazonian jungle's monkeys have prehensile tails that allow them to swiftly move among the trees.

Cebus apella
Black machín

Cebus alfibrons White machín

Caiman crocodylus White caiman

411 species of amphibians
387 species of reptiles

In the Amazonian jungle, there are 28 species of venimous snakes.

The Anaconda is the Amazonian jungle's most feared and mysterious creature. It is considered as the world's largest constrictor boa, as it lacks venom glands, and females can reach 8 meters in length. ▶

(HP) *Eunectes murinus* Anaconda

Geochelone denticulada

Motelo turtle

Many frog species are exploited for human consumption, as their meat has a high protein content. The Junín Frog (*Batrachophrynus macrostomus*) is one of the most appreciated endemic species which is unfortunately in danger of extinction.

Melanosuchus niger Black caiman

The Black Caiman lives in lakes, rivers ▲ and swampy areas.
It is large, as it can reach 8 meters in length and weigh close to 400 kilos.

Arboreal frog (A/P)

(AB) *Iguana iguana* Green iguana

THE ONLY SIX SPECIES THAT WERE DOMESTICATED BY THE ANDEAN MAN

Lama	Alpaca	Guinea pig	Creole duck	Dog	Cochineal

Lama
Ch'aku

Lama
Q'ara

The Lama is the largest, most docile and tame species among South American cameloids.

They can carry between 30 and 70 kilos.

The offspring of the crossbreed between Lama and Alpaca, is known as "Huarizo".

The Huakaya Alpaca's wool is short, curly, thin, abundant and it presents 32 natural colors.

The Suri Alpaca's fiber is curly, shiny and longer (40 cm.), as well as thin and silky.

Peru possesses 80% of the world's South American cameloid population.

Alpaca
Suri

Alpaca
Huakaya

Creole duck

Guinea pig

Researchers state that there were at least two types of dogs: The furry dog, like that of the Lord of Sipan, and the other one, known as the hairless dog or Peruvian dog.

Peruvian dog

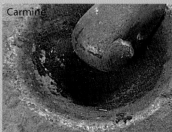

Cochineal

Peru is the first cochineal producing and exporting country, in the world.

The natural colorant extracted from cochineal is very much sought for in the food, cosmetic and pharmaceutical industries.

Carmine

PERUVIAN FLORA

According to the Ministry of Environment, Peru has:

- About 25,000 plant species constituting 10% of the world's total, of which 5,000 are endemic.
- The world record in number of species of trees per hectare of forest.
- More than 1,000 types of ferns.
- More than 180 plant species cultivated by the Andean people.
- A considerable number of plant species that have contributed to world medicine, although many have been patented by foreign companies.

(WH)

Mangrove

(MS) Carob

(WH) Dry forest

Cactus

Molle

Tara

Yareta

Epiphyte

Fungus

Fern

More than 3,000 types of orchids

Epidendrum syringothyrsus

Prosthechea vespa

Phragmipedium caudatum

Lycaste macrophylla

Cyrtochilum minax

Sobralia dichotoma

Telipogon bowmanii

Stanhopea sp.

Anguloa virginalis

Masdevallia aff. antonii

Epidendrum secundum

Trichopilia fragrans

About 650 fruit species

Passion fruit — *Passiflora ligularis*

Annona cherimola — Custard apple

Opuntia Ficus — Tuna

Pacae — *Inga fullei*

Lúcuma

Sancayo

Tumbo

Pouteria obovat

Fam. *Cactaceae*

Passiflora tripartit

Physalis peruviana — Aguaymanto

Elderberry — *Sambucus*

Pepino — *Solanum muricatum*

Qantu or qantuta
Peru's National Flower
Cantua buxifolia

Achanqaray
Begonia veitchii

Choqllo choqllo
Abatia macrophylla

Manayupa
Desmodium vargasianum

Begonia
Begonia bracteosa

Rata rata
Abutilon sylvaticum

Puka sullu
Bomarea coccinea

Fam. Solanaceae

Asnaq sage
Befaria aestuans

Tumbo flower
Passiflora tripartita

Ayaq zapatillan
Fam. scrophulariaceae

Llaulli
Fam. Asteraceae

Rose of the Andes
Befaria aestuans

Nasa poissoniana

Agalinis lanceolata

Paradise Bird
Fam. Strelitziaceae

Alonsoa acutifolia
Aya aya

Costus Acreanus
Caña caña

Fam. Lupinus

Fam. Melastomataceae
Tili tili

Some tubercles and roots

Lepidium meyenii — Maça

Ullucus tuberosus — Olluco or lisas

Smallanthus Sonchifolius — Yacón

Oxalis tuberose — Oca

Xanthosoma sagittifolium — Uncucha

Tropaeolum tuberosum — Año or mashua

Ipomoea batatas — Sweet potato

Arracacia xanthorriza — Virraca

Manihot esculenta — Manioc

Dehydrated potatoes

There are different types of Andean-style dehydrated potatoes obtained by submiting sweet or bitter potatoes to specific techniques. Therefore, these potatoes have different colors and flavors.

Tunta

Chuño

Moraya

Some grains and cereals

Chenopodium quinoa

Quinua

Kiwicha

Amaranthus caudatus

Cañihua
Chenopodium pallidicaule

Zea mays

Purple Corn

Some leguminous plants and cucurbitacea

Tarwi
Lupinus mutabilis

Common Bean

Lima bean
Phaseolus lunatus

Caihua
Cyclanthera pedata

Pumpkin
Cucurbita maxima

Natural areas

Protected natural areas were established, in order to rescue our natural heritage. The National System of Natural Areas protected by the State, is composed of National Parks, National Reserves, National Sanctuaries, Historical Sanctuaries, Hunting Preserves, Protection Forests, Communal Reserves, Landscape Reserves and Reserved Areas. In Peru, there are a total of 67 protected natural areas.

Land according to its aptitude

Soils in Peru present permanent limitations referred to for their characteristics, extreme climatic conditions, risks of erosion and drainage or humidity conditions.

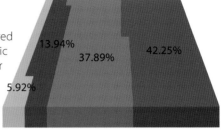

13.94%
37.89%
42.25%
5.92%

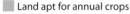 Land apt for annual crops
Pastures
Timber production
Protected land

Source: Ministry of Agriculture

NATURAL PHENOMENA

Due to its geographical location and the negative impact of extreme climatic phenomena, Peru is permanently exposed to a variety of disasters caused by nature, and its vulnerability is accentuated by the global warming effects. Natural phenomena that cause major size disasters are: Earthquakes and the El Niño Phenomenon, although there are others that occur with minor impact than the previous ones, such as river swells, avalanches, landslides, floods, draughts and frosts.

Earthquakes

The direct cause of seismic movements registered on the Peruvian coast, is that of the collision and friction of the Nazca Plate against the base of the South American Continental Plate, which also often produce seaquakes or tsunamis.

Other reasons that cause earthquakes are geological faults in the Andes and volcanic eruptions (Peru is located on the Pacific's Circle of Fire, where 68% of all the world's earthquakes are being registered).

One of the 20th century's most devastating earthquakes occurred in 1970 (Ancash), as it reached a magnitude of 7.8 on the Richter Scale, and was followed by an avalanche that buried 70,000 people.

The most important volcanoes are in the departments of Arequipa, Moquegua and Tacna.

Lloqllas

These are better known as Huaycos. They are water and mud swells loaded with rocks that run along very narrow and steep river basins and are mainly activated by rains.

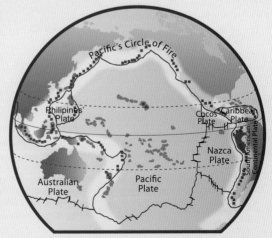

39

THE EL NIÑO PHENOMENON (SOUTH PACIFIC OSCILLATION — ENSO)

This planetary climatic phenomenon has its origin on the North coast of Peru and it generally appears around Christmas time. It is born from the atmospheric pressure's variations and superficial heating of the ocean's waters; that is to say that an alteration produces itself in diverse oceanographic and atmospheric factors which, as a sum, often bring disasters (Especially rains of great intensity). This phenomenon is followed by another opposite one which is known as The Niña, the effects of which are equally devastating

The El Niño Phenomenon is not cyclic, as it can be weak, moderate, strong and extraordinary.

Normal conditions

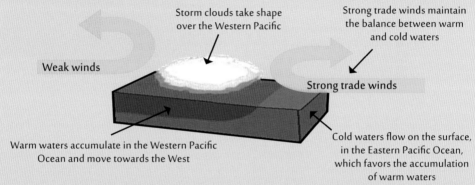

Storm clouds take shape over the Western Pacific

Strong trade winds maintain the balance between warm and cold waters

Weak winds

Strong trade winds

Warm waters accumulate in the Western Pacific Ocean and move towards the West

Cold waters flow on the surface, in the Eastern Pacific Ocean, which favors the accumulation of warm waters

Warming or the El Niño's conditions

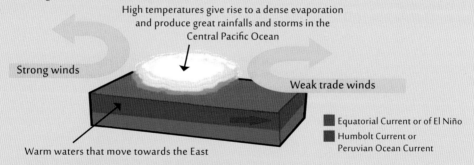

High temperatures give rise to a dense evaporation and produce great rainfalls and storms in the Central Pacific Ocean

Strong winds

Weak trade winds

Warm waters that move towards the East

■ Equatorial Current or of El Niño
■ Humbolt Current or Peruvian Ocean Current

The El Niño phenomenon, and in many cases, the Mega El Niño, as well as devastating rains, abnormal drought, earthquakes and volcanic eruptions protagonized a history of catastrophies,

during which the Andean civilization collapsed a number of times, and was forced to migrate, often taking only its knowledge along. The Andean civilization continued and started its long journey all over again, in one and another different space, increasing its skill in being able to see the past, as well as its adaptation capacity, and above all, that of ever accumulating more and more knowledge that has been the origin and support of its development and power.

HISTORY OF PERU

The chroniclers were the first who intended to write Peru's history, putting emphasis on the Inkas' history.

The chronicles are documents written during the conquest and colony, which contain very valuable Andean information. However, in some cases, they have created confusion and a distortion of history has been originated, due to lack of knowledge, omission or inclusion of certain subjective elements or criteria.

(GPA)

Felipe Guamán Poma De Ayala (1556 - 1644), Peruvian chronicler whose work "New Chronicle and Good Government" is considered as one of the most peculiar in the world's historiography.

Inca Garcilaso de la Vega (1539 - 1616), first half-breed Peruvian personality and great-grandson of Túpaq Inka Yupanqui. In his work "Royal Commentaries of the Incas", he exposes an appreciation of the history of Peru. This work constitutes the base and model of the country's identity, in spite of the existence of certain utopian conceptions.

Peru's history remained almost unchanged 'till the end of the 1950's. From then on, all existing sources and possible testimonies are being studied, and more information sources are still being sought. This is how greater interest has been oriented towards archaeological, ethnological, geological, paleo-climatological researching, etc

Reconstructing the historical process of Peruvian pre-Hispanic societies, putting it into chronological order and giving details on their development's cultural progress, is a very difficult task, being that the latter was not uniform; neither in time, nor in space. However, today, there is an acceptable chronological order.

Peru's history starts with the Pre-Ceramic Stage, followed by the Initial Ceramic Stage, giving way to a chronological sequence which, according to the proposal expressed by J. Rowe, is divided into three time lapses called: "Horizons" (Periods of broad cultural expansion), interrupted by two "Periods" (Moments of development and independent regional tendencies which cohabitated in parallel). In that way, the classification in periods of pre-Columbian past is summarized in the following manner:

Approximation to the Andean past's classification, per phases

I	II	III	IV	V	VI	VII
PRE-CERAMIC STAGE	**INITIAL CERAMIC STAGE**	**EARLY HORIZON**	**EARLY INTERMEDIATE PERIOD**	**MIDDLE HORIZON**	**LATE INTERMEDIATE PERIOD**	**LATE HORIZON**
About 15000 b.C. - 2000 b.C. / 1800 b.C.	2000 b.C. / 1800 b.C. - About 1000 b.C.	About 1000 b.C. - About 200 b.C.	About 200 b.C. - About 500 a.D.	About 500 a.D. - About 900 a.D.	About 900 a.D. - About 1438 a.D.	1438 a.D. - 1532 a.D.
Adaptation of the Andean man	Ceramics appear	Broad cultural expansion	Development and regional tendencies	Broad cultural expansion	Development and regional tendencies	Broad cultural expansion
Paiján Guitarrero Lauricocha Telarmachay Chilca CARAL Waka Prieta etc.	Kotosh Sechín Ancón Cupisnique etc.	CHAVIN	Paracas Pucara Salinar Mochica Nazca Recuay Vicus Lima etc.	TIAWANAKO WARI	Lambayeque Chimú Chachapoyas Chancay Chincha K'illke Lupaka Qolla etc.	INKA

Paiján
Kotosh
Chavin
Mochica
Chimú
Inka
Sechín
Paracas
Tiawanako
Chancay
Caral
Nazca
Wari
K'illke
Chachapoyas
Waka Prieta
Vicus

I.- Pre-Ceramic Stage (About 15000 b.C. - 2000 /1800 b.C.)

- The population's adaptation to the Andean territory took place more than 15,000 years ago.
- The inhabitants settled in river basins and the Quechua Area.
- They were seasonal nomads.
- Groups of hunting and gathering nomads who became evermore selective.
- About 8000 b.C., there already were signs of sedentary settlements, as agricultural and animal raising activities started.
- Around 6000 b.C., the agricultural development propelled monumental architecture, with the construction of sanctuaries and public buildings.
- Close to 3000 b.C., the Andean civilization's first and most ancient urban complex appeared; "The Sacred City of Caral - Supe ".

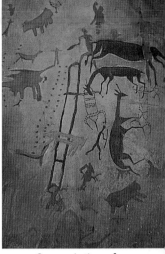

Cave painting of Toquepala, Tacna (9000 b.C.)

II.- Initial Ceramic Stage (About 2000/1800 - 1000 b.C.)

- Ceramics appeared.
- Agriculture was the most important activity for subsistence.
- The temples were attended by priests in charge of astronomical observation.
- The nations lived independently, but kept open communication through profuse interchange.
- The Temple of Chavin de Huantar started to be a concentration point the fame of which was diffused, giving way to a new stage and propelling the development of innovative societies, such as that of Paracas (700 – 200 b.C.).

III.- Early Horizon (About 1000 - 200 b.C.)

- It is characterized by the formation of social classes and diffusion of Chavin's flourishing cult.
- Chavin's successful cult produces the first great regional integration.
- Around 200 b.C., Chavin declines in strength and influence.
- In the transition between that stage and the following one, innovative societies developed such as: Salinar, Viru-Gallinazo, Vicus and Pucará, among others.
- These societies are situated at the dawn of state organizational forms.

IV.- Early Intermediate Period (About 200 b.C. - 500 a.D.)

- It was a stage of regional development and flourishing, during which each social group developed with its own personality.
- These cultures opposed resistance to external influences and made sure not to lose their identity and commercial relations.
- There was a strong stratification of social groups, of the pyramidal type.
- The ceremonial centers and human settlements grew to the point of converting themselves into cities.
- Artistic expression experienced huge development.
- The development of the ecological levels' control system was improved.
- During that stage, societies formed the first states, in the Central Andes, such as: Moche, Nazca, Recuay, Lima, Cajamarca, etc.

Chavin's monolithic "Lanzón" (Long spear): 4.53 meters high

V.- Middle Horizon (About 500 - 900 a.D.)

- It was the second moment of cultural integration and diffusion in the Andean world.
- During that stage, there were two phases: One of autonomous regional development and the other, of great integration, characterized by the cultural diffusion and influence of two outstanding nations: Tiawanako and Wari.
- Both nations peacefully cohabited, on a great territory, up to the point of consolidating a powerful bipolar State, through reciprocity. That State was of a theocratic type.
- Tiawanako appeared way before the Wari and its cultural development included a long time period which got to its apogee in 500 a.D.
- Wari absorbed cultural traits of other nations. That political and religious power developed between the years 600 and 900 a.D.
- Around 1000 a.D., these populations disappeared, leaving deep marks in those they had conquered.

VI.- Late Intermediate Period (About 900 - 1438 a.D.)

- The downfall of the Wari-Tiawanako power originated the regional resurging, during which local cultures flourished that formed lordships and confederations.
- A period of cultural diversity began 'till the arrival of the Inkas. These cultures were: Lambayeque, Chimú, Chancay, Ychma, Callique, Chincha, Chachapoyas, Cajamarca, Wanca, Qolla, Lupaca, Aymara, among others; many of which were later on annexed to the Tawantinsuyo.

VII.- Late Horizon (1438 - 1532 a.D.)

- The last pre-Hispanic stage began with the greatest and most powerful State in the Central Andes, during the Inkan time period.
- Its creators managed to gather and take advantage of the experiences and achievements of nations that preceded them.
- Their tolerance for cultural traits of conquered nations and positive influence by means of different strategies and homogeneous beliefs, allowed them to integrate in great part, the nations that composed the Tawantinsuyo.

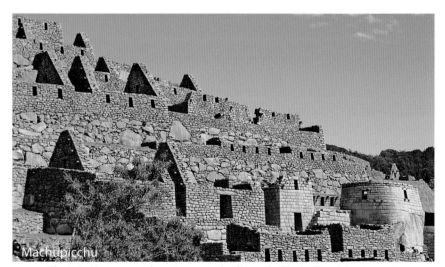

The Late Horizon or Inkan time period collapsed with the Spanish conquest, and thus, a new stage started.

INKAN TIME PERIOD

Before the Inkas' settlement, the ancient inhabitants of the Cusco (Qosqo) Valley, shared the place, establishing different kinds of relationships, pacts and alliances among themselves, in order to achieve a peaceful cohabitation, which seems to have been complicated and difficult.

That is how a primary culture called Marcavalle (1000 b.C.) started to develop, followed by others like the Chanapata (800 b.C.), Qotakalli (600 a.D.) and K'illke (750 a.D. – 1100 a.D.). These were the first cultural manifestations of what would later become the powerful Inkan State which, in addition, inherited the millenary Andean culture; product of community effort and thus, considered as the continuation and synthesis of the Andean trajectory.

Therefore, by the end of the 13th century, Cusco had already converted itself into the most important city at that time, and at the beginning of the 15th century, the development of the greatest and most powerful State on the American continent began with unmistakable features.

The Inkas' origins are getting lost in time and are explained through myths and legends. These reveal that human groups lead by cultural heroes, moved along in search of fertile land to get settled on. Among these Andean chiefs, Manko Qapaq or Ayar Manko stood out, as he settled in the Watanay Valley and founded the Sacred City of Cusco in which the Inkan dynasty was established.

Mythical founders of Cusco **(GPA)**

▲ Manko Qapaq   Mama Oqllo ▼

Territorial expansion and organization

The Inkan expansionist policy responded to the divine order of consolidating the Andean world, with the purpose of uniting nations, civilizing them, putting order among them and implementing an economic system that would allow them to ensure the production of food and cover the needs of the population in growth.

Its grandeur and maximum expansion was achieved almost 100 years after the war against the Chankas; a hostile neighboring nation.

That territory was divided into four regions or suyos, which gave it the name of Tawantinsuyo, with a concept of pure demarcation and the center or capital city of which was Cusco.

The Suyos (Regions of the Inkan State) are still an issue under major research. Regarding their composition or division, it is considered that each Suyo or Region was divided in Wamaní (Provinces or large areas, in varying number) which, in turn, were divided into Saya or Marka (Sectors or smaller areas, in varying number) and each one of these was composed of a varying number of Ayllu (Villages or communities).

It had a territorial extension of 1,731,900 km^2; about 35% larger than the present Peruvian territory, located between 2° 04'18" of latitude North and 35° 06' 09" of latitude South; that is to say, from the Ancasmayo or Blue River, in the region of Pasto – Columbia, to the Bio Bio and Maule rivers (Today's Puerto Constitución), in Chile, which, in a straight line between both points, comes to 4,240 km. in length.

Military power

The Inkan State had an active and strictly organized military life (With a relatively precarious system, in comparison with stable military organizations) which contributed to its fast territorial expansion. Although, more than with the use of force, they resorted to a series of strategies to consolidate their conquests, like, for example, tolerance, persuasiveness, negotiation, generosity, pleas, kindness, gifts, alliances; in short, a whole diplomatic skill, for a resolvent adhesion.

Capital city
Qollasuyo
Antisuyo
Kuntisuyo
Chinchaysuyo

This new State's efficient functioning demanded an intelligent organization imparted by a ruling elite specialized in management.

None of the conquered nations were taken into slavery, but rather, became one more province of the territory, in which the Inka's power and authority were imposed.

Each Suyo or Region was divided in Wamaní (Provinces or large areas, in varying number) which, in turn, were divided into Saya or Marka (Sectors or smaller areas, in varying number) and each one of these was composed of a varying number of Ayllu (Villages or communities).

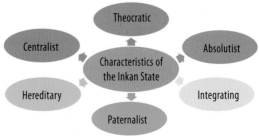

Approximation to the Inkan Social Organization

The Inkan social structure was rigid, in relation to other ethnic groups.

Royalty

• Inka

The titles of the Son of the Sun were: Inka, Sapan Inka or Intiq Churin. He was of semi-divine condition, generous and donor of essential products in the Andean economy. As such, he was at the top of the Inkan social pyramid.

INKA: Name used as a generic caste denomination and at present, the designation Inka is applied, by extension, to the country or State and to its people.

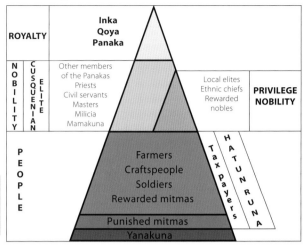

Social Pyramid proposal
based on the information of F. Kauffmann.

Note that the words brother / sister also refer to the people who belonged to the same generation.

• Qoya (The Inka's spouse)

She was the Inka's legitimate and main spouse, and was· also called Daughter of the Sun and Moon. As a consequence, she was considered as the Inka's sister.

• Panaka (Matrilineal Royal Family)

It was formed by the descendants of each Inka.
The Panaka had to fulfill the mission of telling the remembrances of its already defunct Sapan Inka.
The Inka's mummy had the faculty and right to go on intervening in the Tawantinsuyo's political life, through its Panaka.

Nobility

It was efficient and very useful to the State, due to its knowledge in administrative management and planning, and was divided in two groups:

• Cusco's elite or blood nobility

All of Cusco's nobles who belonged to the Panakas, and occupied different positions related to power were considered as such. They were civil servants, priests, masters and militia who had to behave in an impeccable way, worthy of being taken as an example.

• The privilege nobility

• The local elites or provincial nobles were a group constituted by very important ethnic chiefs who contributed to the Tawantinsuyo's organizational balance.
• The nobles prized or rewarded for some merit or special service to the State.

The Inka and Qoya were carried on a litter. (GPA)

| The elite also practised cranial deformation. | Only the elite (Royalty and Nobility) practised polygamy. | Likewise, they deformed their ear lobes in an exaggerated way; reason for which the Spanish called them "big ears". |

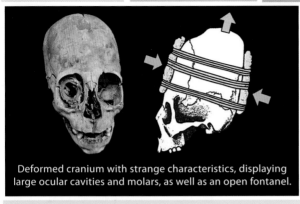

The Andean elites were accustomed to deforming their cranium, for aesthetic and differentiating purposes. It is also probable that they did it with the intention of influencing brain functions.

These techniques were applied on infants at an early age, on the basis of anatomic knowledge and according to the shape that was to be given to the cranium.

Deformed cranium with strange characteristics, displaying large ocular cavities and molars, as well as an open fontanel.

The first deformed cranium found in Peru, belonged to an individual who lived around 6,000 years b.C.

The people or popular classes

- **Hatun runa** (Men from the people)

It was the group of peasants, shepherds and artisans who were considered as productive men who, after having accomplished their military service and gotten married, converted themselves into tax payers, as much of products, as of personal work.

They were organized in Ayllus; villages or groups of monogamous families who believed they descended from a common mythical ancestor, united by reciprocity, solidarity and cooperative work relationships.

• Mitma or mitimae

It was the resident, transposed or removed people.

This was an eminently political system, to ensure dominion, through which groups of people or families were transferred, for a determined period of time, to work and live in areas that were not theirs. There were two types of mitma:

1. Those who were transferred as a reward and with the aim of showing good example and teach.
2. Those who went under punishment, to ensure their insertion in the Tawantinsuyo. Depending on their conduct, these could go back to their place of origin.

• Yana or yanakuna

They were people who were disconnected from their ayllu.

The work they performed was varied, as they especially served in domestic tasks and were exempted from taxes. Therefore, they had no Kuraka (Chief) and were excluded from the reciprocity system. Close contact with the high hierarchy, lead certain yanakuna to nobility.

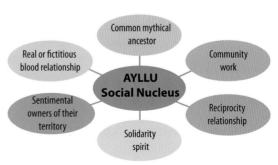

PACHAKUTEQ (1438 – 1471 a.D.)

In quechua, this name literally means "The World's Reformer" or "World's Transformer".

He was the Ninth Inka and is considered as the ancient American world's greatest statesman. He was the founder of the Tawantinsuyo which he organized and he was dedicated to its efficient administration.

Some examples of his work:

- He is attributed with the victory in the war against the Chanka, which opened the way for the conquest, as well as for the political and economic dominion and control of other nations, and expansion of the territory.
- He achieved many construction works and among them, stands out the embellishment of the city of Cusco, giving it the shape of a puma, the reconstruction of the Temple of the Sun or Qorikancha, the planning and beginning of the construction of Machupicchu, the building of paths, bridges, warehouses, benched terraces, irrigation canals, etc.
- He set the functions of administrative, political, military and religious civil servants.
- He dictated laws.
- He established the social hierarchy.
- He established the solar calendar, with 12 month years.

Inka Pachakuteq (M/M)

TUPAQ INKA YUPANKI (1471 – 1493 a.D.)

He is considered as a great warrior, excellent administrator, planner, expert in the management of human resources, and man of great personality who ruled in accordance with his father's government policy.

During the Inkan period, the greatest expansion of the Tawantinsuyo's road network was achieved.

WAYNA QAPAQ (1493 – 1525 a.D.)

He made great efforts to consolidate the Inkan dominion and lead the Tawantinsuyo to its maximum extension and development. His death, as well as that of his already appointed successor, Ninan Kuyuchi, was caused by smallpox, an illness unknown in the New World.

APPROXIMATION TO THE INKAN SUCCESSION

		Qapaqkuna / Inkas	Panakas	Chronology	Dynasties
Le g e n d a r y		LOCAL PHASE			Urin Qosqo 1st Dynasty
	1	Manko Qapaq	Chima Panaka	1200 a.D.	
	2	Sinchi Roka	Raura Panaka	1230	
	3	Lloq'e Yupanki	Auayni Panaka	1260	
	4	Mayta Qapaq	Usca Mayta Panaka	1300	
	5	Qapaq Yupanki	Apo Mayta Qapaq Panaka	1320	
	6	Inka Roka	Vicaquirao Panaka	1350	
	7	Yawar Waqaq	Aucaylli Panaka	1380	Hanan Qosqo 2nd Dynasty
	8	Wiraqocha Inka	Sucsu Panaka	1410	
Hi s t o r i c a l		EXPANSION PHASE			
	9	Pachakuteq	Hatun Ayllu Panaka	1438	
	10	Tupaq Yupanki	Qapaq Ayllu Panaka	1471	
	11	Wayna Qapaq	Tumipampa Panaka	1493	
	12	Waskar		1525	
	13	Atawallpa		1532	
No m i n a t i v e		COLONIAL PHASE			
	14	Thopa Wallpa		1533	
	15	Manko Inka		1536	
	16	Sayri Tupaq		1542	
	17	T'itu Kusi Yupanki		1557	
	18	Tupaq Amaru		1568 - 1572	
List of Inkas with the best acceptation for researchers					

Approximation to the Inkan Political Organization

The extended territory required hierarchical and functional structure, in which the presence of a numerous dominant elite would stand out.

For the good management and administration of the State, there was a group of civil servants appointed by the Inka, with clearly established functions. These did not seek monopoly or concentration of wealth, but rather, they collaborated in the purpose of optimizing the planning for greater food production.

• Inka (Maximum Authority)

In his condition of semi-divine being, chosen by his Father the Sun, to rule, he was the maximum authority who exercised the mission of giving welfare and security to the people (In exchange of their work, obedience and faithfulness), considering the city of Cusco as the center of the Tawantinsuyo.

A diarchy existed, given the principles of duality and complementarity. In political matters (Power related to the State's expansion, order and administrative tasks), it took place with the successor of the ruling Sovereign, and in the religious entourage (Ritual tasks the role of which was transcendental, in the State's social and political organization), with the High Priest.

• Auki (Prince, Heir to the Throne)

It is the denomination given to the Inka's sons who had the opportunity to show their ability to rule.

• Tawantinsuyo Kamachiq (Imperial Council)

It was integrated by authorities of the highest hierarchy, representatives of the Hanan and Urin Qosqo and of the Four Regions or Tawantinsuyo, called the Apokuna or Suyuyuqkuna dedicated to counselling the Inka.

As M. Rostworowski says, there was the "right of the most skillful one". The chosen heir to assume power, was the most capable, talentuous, intelligent and audacious. In order to get initiated and introduce himself into the world of State governing, and demonstrate his virtues, he had to very actively participate in its process.

Royal Council / (GPA)

• Apunchiq (Representative of the Inka)

He was in charge of ruling over a region, subject to the Tocrikoq's supervision. He would ensure order and the fulfilling of regulations. He had political and military attributions.

• Toqrikoq o Tukuy Rikuq (Supervisor)

He was the special supervisor and administrator. His function was to enforce the rules in the provinces, in coordination with the Apunchiq. As an inspector, he had the authority to impose punishments, resolve conflicts, celebrate weddings and collect taxes.

• Kuraka (Chief)

He was the Chief and was in charge of an ethnic group or ayllu, and had the obligation of organizing the people and to serve as a mediator between it and the authorities.

The Kurakas were of different categories and obeyed hierarchies, in accordance with the geographical area and/or quantity of population they had under their command.

The Tawantinsuyo's Administrative Organization

For the Inkan State's efficient administration, a system was required that would allow an adequate information of needs, problems and resources, in order to facilitate proper decision making, which was possible, thanks to the organization and decimal based division system.

The decimal based administration

For the control of the population and tax system to be efficient, the Inkas thought of a form of social organization and division which was registered in the khipus, as exact accounting records.

This ordering system was based on decimal computation and its half, according to necessity. Therefore, the men from the people were divided into groups of ten, one hundred, one thousand and ten thousand heads of family. In that way, the population's decimal organization had as its base the head of one family called Pureq.

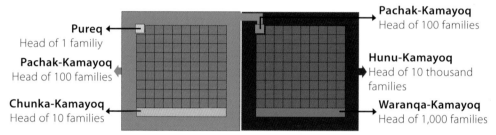

Pureq ←
Head of 1 familiy

Pachak-Kamayoq
Head of 100 families

Chunka-Kamayoq
Head of 10 families

Pachak-Kamayoq
Head of 100 families

Hunu-Kamayoq
Head of 10 thousand families

Waranqa-Kamayoq
Head of 1,000 families

According to the Major Royal Academy of Quechua Language, the meaning of "Kamayoq", is: Specialist or expert who has the authority or dominion over something, with full knowledge of it.

INKAN ORGANIZATIONAL STRUCTURE PROPOSAL

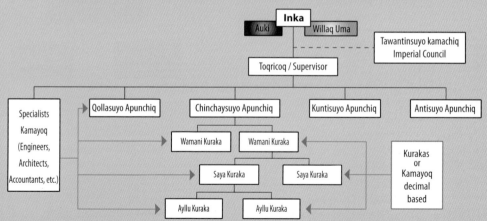

The State's fast expansion originated new challenges which had to be faced, creating adequate administration systems and hiring required civil servants of different hierarchies and skills.

The specialists (Kamayoq) coordinated the execution of projects and works for the State, directly with the authorities pertinent to the level (Suyo, Wamani, Saya or Ayllu), in the place where labor had to be developed. With this project system, they hastened the State's decimal based political, administrative and burocratic division.

Various handwritten annotations surround the illustration.

(GPA)

Population of the Tawantinsuyo

Peru's difficult geography determined a population distributed in ethnic groups, with their own customs, artistic expressions, language and religion. This is how they enjoyed certain autonomy, with the condition of accepting and practicing certain impositions of the Inkan State, in the aim of achieving common goals and always strengthening the assimilation and integration process.

It is impossible to manifest the exact number of the Tawantinsuyo's population, but the quantity of construction works produced in such a short time, leads us to believe that it fluctuated between 8 and 16 million inhabitants.

The official language

The official language was the Runasimi which means "The Man's Talk", better known as Quechua and its learning was mandatory, in order to ease communication, as well as the natives' integration process.

Moralist State

F. Kauffmann sustains that the Inkan people were clearly moralists.

The population had to observe norms of conduct, as much in the moral aspects, as in what was related to governmental or public precepts. If the people committed an infraction, they were punished in a severe and immediate way.

Education

Education in a systematic way was only for the elite's young people.

For the young men, it was given by the Amautas, in the House of Knowledge or Yachay Wasi,

F. Kauffmann says: "Crimes were considered as offences to the State, but not to divinities"

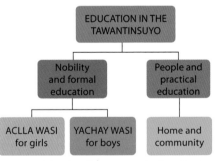

EDUCATION IN THE TAWANTINSUYO

Nobility and formal education — People and practical education

ACLLA WASI for girls | YACHAY WASI for boys | Home and community

without the need for formal writing. The intention was to combine intelligence and talent, in the art of ruling and performing high level administrative tasks. It was complemented with studies on religion, astronomy, engineering, medicine, accounting, history, etc.

Young noble girls, as well as girls selected among the people, were educated under the Mamakunas' orientation, in the House of the Chosen Women or Aklla Wasi, where they learned diverse forms of art and activities, such as, for example: The confection of fine products, preparation of meals, elaboration of the chicha or aqha (Germinated and fermented corn drink), etc., as well as serving the cult to the Sun God, the Inka, aristocracy and in festivities.

The half-breed chronicler Inca Garcilaso de la Vega attributes the following statement to Inka Roka: "The people should not be taught what should only be known by great figures". Therefore, education or formal knowledge was only for the elite and served the State's interests.

The akllas were women chosen since early childhood. Their category and functions were different: Some were exclusively dedicated to worshipping the Sun God (Inti), others could be the Inka's concubines, and others still, could be gifted, in order to strengthen alliances.

Women performed a proactive and fundamental role in every one of the Andean culture's historical moments.

Their presence was recognized and considered as very necessary and complementary to the male role. Therefore, they also participated in hierarchical and ruling positions.

Education was based on good example, which made it so that the Inkan people cultivated virtues like: Hard work, veracity, honesty, obedience, respect, peace and joyfulness.

Inkan writing

There were no findings of written texts with alphabetical or syllabic signs, but there are elements that contain varied information such as: The khipus, tokapus, quelqas and the abacus or yupana, that can be considered as a form of writing.

• The khipu

It was an ingenious and fundamental instrument that worked like a codified writing which served as a helper to memorize data (Mnemonic tool), for the registry of quantitative and qualitative information.

The relation between the colors, types of knots, the distance between them, the length of the string, etc., held data related to the calendar, population's potential,

(M/M)

The chronicler Agustino Calancha mentioned: "To know how to count and understand quipus… was their way of writing".

(MD)

The khipukamayoq or specialists in the handling of khipus, were indispensable for the State's administration.

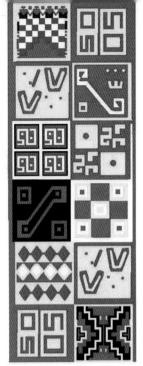

Tokapu

the quantity of production, resources, number of soldiers, memorable events, history and much more. But, the only one who could compose, keep and decipher them was the one in charge or khipukamayoq.

- **The tokapus**

    They were successively ordered frames, with variable designs from rectangle to rectangle, which could represent words or information codes, and they appear on keros or vessels and woven fabrics.

- **The qelqas**

    These were designs or paintings, although their concept is equivalent to writing in English. Xylography is part of the qelqas.

- **The yupanas**

    Also known as abacus, they were instruments with square boxes which corresponded to decimal units.

M. Rostworowski says that to all of this is added the custom of narrating history and praising the ancestors' feats, during certain ceremonies, with the purpose of guaranteeing a "collective memory".

Upon the Spaniards' arrival, the Inkan nobility remembered their ancestors for several past generations.

Economy

The basis of Inkan economy was agriculture and the administration of the abundant production, mainly complemented by animal breeding, fishing and textile work. It was backed up by a food and goods conservation and storage system interconnected by a gigantic road network.

Principles of Inkan economy

One of the most important concerns was that of satisfying the basic needs and alimentation of the whole population surrounded by a hostile natural environment.

The Inkas used certain mechanisms to increase their food production and distribute it, so as to achieve general welfare in that way.

- **Reciprocity** was an institutionalized ordering social and economic principle in the Andean world, with rules, as well as general and traditional procedures. It consisted in the interchange based on the offering and receiving of goods and services among the members of a village or ayllu and on those of the Inkan State, as the mediating element or in order to get favors, along with the strengthening of cooperation alliances. Therefore, fulfilling the reciprocity protocol was strict and definitely included hospitality, with gifts, food and drinks. This also happened on the religious level.

Reciprocity played a fundamental part in the process of assimilation and consolidation of the Tawantinsuyo.

- **Redistribution** was generalized, thanks to great surplus in the production generated by the huge labor force the Inkan State had access to. That production was destined to be stored and redistributed, thus ensuring the population with the State's support and protection; especially in times of need, in addition of being used to control the reciprocity networks.

Work

There was a work community with a general, mandatory, alternating, varied, limited, collective and proportionate character, in accordance with gender and age. Laziness was considered as a crime in offence to the State and therefore, was punished.

Work systems

Taking the criteria of reciprocity and redistribution into consideration, there were three forms of work:

- **The ayni** was the basic form of interchange of services, in order to alleviate urgent needs within the family or the ayllu. It had to be returned in an opportune way.

- **The mink'a** was the collective task performed by all family members or the ayllu, for a common benefit.

- **The mita** was a kind of work that benefited the State and religion. It was performed in rotating shifts and all adults of the ayllu were obliged to participate. The mita was perfectly programmed and it contemplated the individuals' skills and capacities, which

> There was no money, market, commerce or taxes as these are conceived today.

> *"Ama Q'ella, Ama Llulla, Ama Sua"*
> "Don't be lazy, Don't be a lier, Don't be a thief"

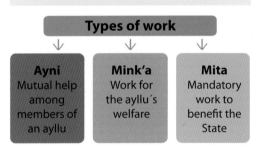

lead them to a certain level of specialization. Its time period varied according to the specific circumstances and requisites, as well as to the place which could be within or outside the ayllu. Upon occasions, the work group could be transferred to very distant places and come back to its village of origin, once their work was done.

Agriculture

The Inkan civilization was, by excellence, an agrarian society which reached its maximum level of evolution, and generated stock surplus, as had never been achieved before in the Andean world.

Nature's challenge, the rough topography, scarce agricultural land and food demand of a growing population, required daring efforts and lead to

> They took advantage of the Islands' bird and bat droppings, as well as of the dung of domestic animals, etc., to keep soils always fertile.

> The Inkas managed to develop a permanent agricultural area of about seven million hectares, of which the benched terrace system constitutes an average of 28%.

the use of diverse technological resources; many of which were already known, and among these, the following stand out:

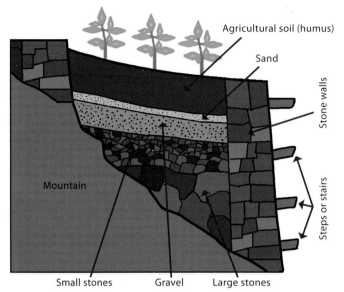

Agricultural soil (humus)

Sand

Stone walls

Steps or stairs

Mountain

Small stones   Gravel   Large stones

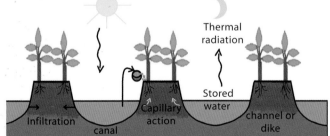

Thermal radiation

Stored water

Capillary action

Infiltration   canal   channel or dike

- **Pata pata**
  (Benched terraces)

  These are multi-functional constructions, as, in addition of broadening agricultural land, they allow the handling of several altitudinal levels, in order to create varied ecosystems and take advantage of the biological diversity. Furthermore, they fulfill a defensive function, as contention walls, and keep the terrain from erosion, landslides, floods, etc.

  Many of these agricultural terraces have a controlled irrigation system and others are irrigated by rains or the fogs' condensation.

- **Hoyas**
  (Excavated fields)

  These are excavations made in arid areas, to reach down to underground humid layers that are convenient for agriculture.

- **Waru waru**
  (Marshland fields)

  It is an efficient system for the handling of soil and water, in flat floodable marshlands that create a thermal effect which protects the crops from frost, in addition of optimizing the soil's quality.

Some work tools

Chira   Rauk'ana   Chakitakllas

The inkan animal raising activities

It was another significant activity. They lead lamas and alpacas to pasture. In addition, they raised ducks and guinea pigs.

The cuy or qoe *(Cavia porcellus)* is a rodent the meat of which is a source of proteins superior to that of other meats. Likewise, it contains essential fats that transform into Arachidonic fatty Acid (AA) and Docosahexaenoic fatty Acid (DHA) which are important for the development of brain neurons and protection of cellular membranes.

CLASSIFICATION OF THE CAMELOIDS

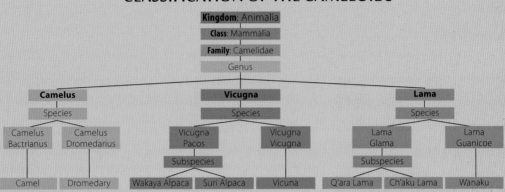

Q'ara Lama

Ch'aku Lama

Suri Alpaca

Wanaku

Among the South American cameloids, there are: The lama, alpaca, wanaku and vicuna.

The lama *(Lama glama)*: It was very useful, and the Andean people's only burden animal. Along with the others, it offered its wool, meat, leather, bones and dung. There are two species: Ch'aku y Q'ara.

The alpaca *(Lama pacos)*: There are two species: Wakaya and Suri. It is raised especially for the production of wool, as it has great worldwide prestige.

The wanaku *(Lama guanicoe)*: It is a wild and endangered species.

the vicuna *(Vicugna vicugna)*: It is a wild species appreciated for its wool which is the finest in the world. It is called "Gold of the Andes".

Wakaya Alpaca

Vicuna

57

Cumbemayo channel
Cajamarca culture

Inkan canal – Ollantaytambo

Inkan well – Cusco

Hydraulic engineering

The unequal distribution of water on the Peruvian territory motivated the Andean people in developing a real hydraulic science.

The inkas enjoyed great prestige for their vast knowledge on the utilization of water, which helped in their expansion and domination policy.

They were experts in controling water, thanks to their conservation policy, as well as in the perfecting and spreading of extraordinary techniques that allowed them to take water to inaccessible places.

Dams, canals, aqueducts, communicating vessel systems, siphons, artesian wells, artificial lagoons, river deviations, etc., were built, ensuring the supply of water everywhere; be it in villages or agricultural areas.

Qolqas (Grain deposits / warehouses) ◘

The Inkas planned their agricultural and animal raising activities, thinking about getting a better production quality and quantity. As they had surplus, a unique and efficient accumulation, conservation and distribution system was implemented. These warehouses, the structure of which was related to their content and conservation purposes, were strategically located all over the territory, constituting a source of replenishing during draughts, heavy rains, wars, earthquakes, etc. It is considered as the most perfect deposit and replenishing system among all ancient civilizations.

The qolqas, for their number and kinds of deposits, volume and the variety of food and things they contained, were object of awe among the conquerors who took advantage of them during many years after the conquest.

Their total storage capacity is calculated to have been of about 2 million m³ which, in synthesis, represented the core of the State's economic power.

Undoubtedly, there was a tendency of thinking about a long term future, within the understanding that the human being is always at the mercy of nature.

Medicine

The practice of medicine was linked to religion and magic, as the Inkas considered that illnesses had their origin in fright or curses which had to be treated with plants, water, animals and minerals, the properties of which are magical and medicinal. In addition, during the treatment process, it was necessary to perform a series of magical and ritual acts, with prayers, chants, etc.

CRANIAL TREPANATIONS

- These are high precision and dexterity operations; a prodigy in the history of medicine.
- The Andean practitioners had an advanced knowledge of anatomy and displayed an impressive dexterity and precision in this complex and delicate task.
- Patients were operated, who had suffered cranial traumas, especially, as well as those who had migraines or tumors.
- The technique consisted in scrapings, cuts and perforations.
- They used surgical instruments such as scalpels, knives, separators, chisels, spoons, pliers or tweezers, needles, etc., made of metal, obsidian, etc. In the same way, they used dressings, gauze, cotton compresses, bandages, etc.
- They knew the plants' healing and anaesthetic properties, among which the coca leaf stood out.
- The operation was performed "live", with a high percentage of survival, as the regeneration of the bone tissue shows it. Others show that post mortem practices were performed as part of a funerary rite.
- It was performed since the Paracas culture and on to the Inkan Period.

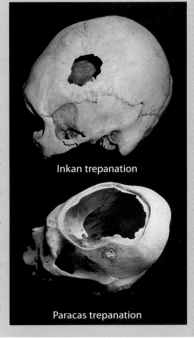

Inkan trepanation

Paracas trepanation

This "Inkan dental prothesis" was found during excavations performed in Muyuqmarka – Saqsaywaman, a great Inkan architectural complex situated on top of a hill, North-west of the city of Cusco.

This is a false tooth carved in stone, which was perfectly set like an implant, under the wisdom tooth.

Magical plants

They used many plants with special properties, as well as magical, religious and medicinal purposes, among which the coca leaf stands out, along with the ayawaska which is based on a kind of vine (*Banisteriopsis caapi*), and the San Pedro (*Trichocereus pachanoi*) cactus.

◀ Small Tiawanako wooden board for the inhalation of psychoactive substances

Chavin sculpture ▶

Astronomy

That science played a crucial part in the displaying of the State's authority.

The Inkas studied the cosmos and its laws, with much interest. They were motivated by the wish to communicate with other species, identify themselves with nature and use it wisely, as a political and religious expression.

The observation of the movements, rising and setting positions of celestial bodies, as well as the projections of light and shadows produced by different objects, allowed them to keep account of the passing of the year, control of time, identification of the seasons, and this lead them to the programming and regulation of social, agricultural and religious events.

The weather forecast and its variations, through astronomical observation, was an exclusive and decisive kind of information managed by the elite. Thus, the knowledge of when, what, how and where to sow, was a source of power.

One of the most observed constellations, to predict weather forecasts, was the Pleiades.

The knowledge of the moments for the Zenith and Nadir also helped in the elaboration of a very efficient calendar, for the development and success of agricultural and livestock raising activities.

The Inkas observed two kinds of constellations: Constellations of shiny stars and dark constellations (The Dark Nebulous Clouds or Coal Sacks) which look like empty spaces within the Milky Way or Hatun Mayu (Great River).

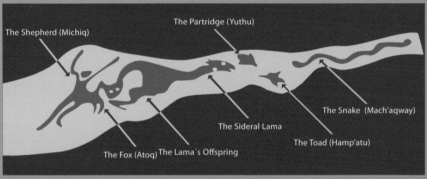

The Shepherd (Michiq)

The Partridge (Yuthu)

The Snake (Mach'aqway)

The Sideral Lama

The Toad (Hamp'atu)

The Fox (Atoq)   The Lama´s Offspring

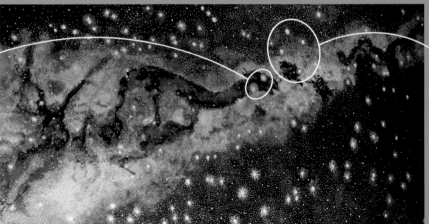

Alpha and Beta Centaurus/ Llamaq Ñawin

Southern Cross / Chakana

The Inkan calendar

The Inkas developed and used a practical, simple and functional solar calendar, integrating the lunar phases and apparition of determined stellar constellations.

The Inkan calendar had 12 solar months and each one of them would have contained 30 or 31 days. Each month included the celebration of festivities and feasts related to some stage of the agricultural activities, as well as religious festivities. Astronomical observations were motives for different ceremonies, and mainly, those associated with solstices and equinoxes.

INKAN RELIGIOUS CEREMONIAL CALENDAR (GPA)

June	July	August	September
October	November	December	January
February	March	April	May

The Inkan State's religious calendar was full of sacred ceremonies and festivities at the same time.

THE AGRICULTURAL CALENDAR (GPA)

August	September	October	November
December	January	February	March
April	May	June	July

The agricultural calendar allowed them:

To know what to sow: Selection of seeds.

Where to sow: Selection of soils.

When and how they had to sow: Assistance and resources, in each phase of the sowing and harvesting processes.

What part of the plant was to be used: How and when to take advantage of the production.

How and where the product had to be stored.

INTI RAYMI (The Sun's Festivity)

It was the most important and solemn festivity performed in honor to the Sun God, as a thanksgiving for the kindness received and as a petition for prosperity; especially to have better harvests.

The Inti Raymi was celebrated on each winter solstice (Southern hemisphere) and required the meticulous organization of each rite, like the sacrifice of the lama, in the entrails of which the Tawantinsuyo's future was predicted, the lighting up of the sacred fire, the presentation of the different offerings, such as chicha and bread, to then, end in a great spree, with songs and dances.

During that celebration, the mummies' presence was indispensable, as well as that of their respective panakas.

CORPUS CHRISTI (Latin) The Celebration of Christ's Body

That festivity is a clear sample of syncretism. This is how no one knows where one religion starts and where the other ends. It is a manifestation of the mixture of the profane and religious worlds, as it reminds us of the Sun's Celebration and replaces it by the cult to the Saints and Virgins. It is celebrated between May and June.

San Jerónimo

The typical dish during the celebration of Corpus Christi (Body of Christ), is the "chiri uchu" which contains oven-baked guinea pig, chicken, corn omelette, cheese, toasted corn, red hot pepper, sausage, algae, "cau cau" and smoked meat.

The Inkan vision of the cosmos

The Inkas had their own conception and interpretation of time and space, with a deep religious feeling.

• Time and space

The concept of time was not linear, but rather circular and/or cyclical. Therefore, what was behind served to name the future and vice versa.

As much for time, as for space, there were:

1. Kay - The present and here.

2. Qhepa - The future and behind.

3. Ñaupa - The past and up ahead.

These three levels are identified with the following sacred animals: The Condor, Puma and Serpent.

• The division of the universe

In turn, they divided the universe into three interrelated environments:

1. Hanaq Pacha

The Upper World or place the Gods have their abode in.

2. Kay Pacha

The World of Here and of the present, where human beings live and which, in turn, could also be the point of union or t'inkuy, between the other two levels.

3. Ukhu Pacha

The Inner and/or Subterranean World, where the ancestors and the force of fertility dwell.

• Duality or yanantin / masintin

The duality concept is another very important parameter in the Andean cosmo - vision. It was an ordering and organizing principle, to set standards between the Andean people's relations and those they had with their external world.

Yanantin and/or masintin are the unitary pair of opposite polarities which are altogether complementary, inseparable, integrating, inter-dependent and part of hierarchies, and their roles can be interchangeable, on the basis of reciprocity.

1. Hanan - The World Above, the right hand, what is male, the positive, etc.
2. Urin - The World Below, the left hand, what is female, the passive, etc.

Yanantin generates the principles of tri-partition and quatri-partition. The idea of quatri-partition, as a duplication of duality, explains the reproduction of space in the urban establishments and the existence of the Four Regions or Tawantinsuyo.

This is the best known shape of the Chakana or Andean Cross which was a very important symbol in the Andean cosmo-vision, and represents the Universe, the Pachamama or Mother Earth, the different shapes of crosses mankind observed in the sky, as well as many other ideological manifestations of the Andean world.

Inkan religious cosmo-vision

The complex geography that presents scarce agricultural soils which depend on rainfalls, originated a particular way of understanding reality, as the Inkas considered the world in which they lived, as a place that was under the decisive influence of numerous gods and sacred entities. This is why, in order to ensure themselves the permanent protection of these gods, they had to perform a series of forms of cult, with rites and offerings, on altars and in temples built all over the Tawantinsuyo.

Their religion was one of the most important political strategies the Inkas used for their expansion and government. The cult also was closely linked to agriculture, with the aim of favoring a good production that would guarantee survival; that is to say, their religion was a practical and functional support philosophy.

Scene on a "kero" (Inkan ceremonial vessel) which represents a ceremony of reciprocity in which the Sun, political divinity imposed by the Inka Pachakuteq, occupies a preferential place, as the synthesis of existence.

The Inkas imposed determined religious patterns, and the cult to the Sun was made official, without eliminating the conquered nations' religious conceptions. Therefore, a great number of divinities that lived in the Heavens and on Earth cohabited, such as celestial bodies, geographical accidents, atmospheric phenomena, mummified ancestors, animals... In short, the Inkas believed that all things had a spirit (Ancient animist tradition) worthy of great respect and veneration. Among the main Inkan divinities, we have:

Inti Tayta (Father Sun)
The Sun enjoyed a preferential place among divinities, being the fertilizing and vivifying god by excellence, source of Power, being considered as the Father of the Inkas and Husband of the Moon.

Mama Killa (Mother Moon)
Mother of the Inkas and very important divinity which inspired them in the elaboration of a calendar used in their agricultural activities.

Ch'aska / Qoyllur (The Stars)
These divinities, considered as the Moon's siblings, were observed to foresee the weather. Among them, the Southern Cross and the Pleiades or Qolqa were the most venerated. (Venus also was an important divinity).

The Andean gods' attributes

They have their own life and soul	They are sexed	They complement each other
They also have power	They are sacred	They deserve respect and devotion
They are perceptible	They respond to petitions	They maintain balance and harmony between nature and human beings

65

Illapa (The Lightning)

Illapa was one of the most reverenced divinities, as it was one of the key agents in food production, and at the same time, it was feared, because it could unleash catastrophes (Hail and excessive rain are worse, and their absence was more terrible still for harvests).

It was considered as one of the manifestations of the divinity of water.

K'uychi (The Rainbow)

It was the closest celestial divinity to mankind, and was associated with the snake, rain and Sun.

Pachamama (Mother Earth)

The importance of the agricultural activity made it so that Mother Earth was considered as one of the fundamental divinities, as the Inkas considered it as their Mother who they adapted themselves to, respecting and venerating it, as it was their life support, and their success and survival depended on it. It was symbolized by the stair-like sign.

Mamaqocha (Mother or origin of water or the Ocean)

This divinity, as well as streams, rivers, lakes and the ocean symbolized the abundance of water and represented a place of origin or Paqarina. Its symbols are seashells and marine snails.

Apu (The Spirits of the mountains)

They are the spirits of mountains and snow-capped peaks to which worshipping had to be rendered, in order to enjoy their protection.

Mallki (The Mummies) ❶

These are the mummified ancestors, venerated as protectors, who participated, especially in festivities, taking part and receiving homage of remembrance and gratefulness.

Waka (The Sacred)

It was the closest and permanent link between the Andean people and the sacred. It could be anything; something transcendental or extraordinary. It was an object of great veneration.

Paqarina
(Places of Human Origins)

These were special kinds of Wacas, as they could be caves, lagoons, mountains, etc.

MUMMIFICATION IN THE ANDES

It was a special technique and process that allowed an excellent state of conservation of the bodies pertaining to members of the dominant class. It was possibly done with the intention of making them immortal.

The Andean man was seeking a place that gathered the propitious environmental conditions for the dehydration and conservation of cadavers that might or not have benefitted from a previous mummification treatment.

For corpses submitted to artificial mummification, they used a variety of techniques for bowel elimination and applications of different plant or mineral substances, etc., and in that way, they avoided putrefaction.

The Andeans believed that there was a world in which life went on after death, and where the dead had the same needs as when they were alive, reason for which they were buried with food, work tools, personal clothes, etc.

As a product of the elites' philosophical thought, which was not available to lay people, there also existed an invisible god or spiritual gods such as WIRAQOCHA who was an abstract divinity who had many names and titles.

More than a creating divinity, Wiraqocha was a superior divinity that ordered an already existing reality or it was omnipresent in what was ordered.

THE "QELQA" OF THE QORIKANCHA

The "Qelqa" is a panel drawn by Juan Santa Cruz Pachacuti, in his chronicle titled "Ancient Relations of this Kingdom of Peru" written around 1613.

The content of this panel, interprets, in great part, the Inkan cosmo-vision or religion which, in turn, organizes the guidelines of their gods' commandments for a balanced cohabitation and good government of the Tawantinsuyo. It possibly was situated in one of the enclosures of the Qorikancha or Temple of the Sun, in Cusco.

HANAQ
* Inti or Sun.
* Celestial body (Venus) - Ch'aska Qoyllor, Achachi Ururi: Bright star. This is the morning star (Venus) which might possibly represent the first ruler: Inka Manko Qapaq.
* Summer- Suksu.
* Chakana in general (Southern Cross and other crosses), which represents duality´s link.
* Saramanka (Pot of Corn): Possible representation of harvest.
* Katachillay, Star which could be the representation of livestock reproduction.
* Chuki Illa or Illapa: Lightning and representation as the god of rain.

KAY
* K'uychi, Turomanya: Sky´s Bow (Rainbow)
* Pacha Mama: The World or Earth.
* Man (Man / Woman: They would be the representation of the Inka and Qoya who, in turn, would symbolize humanity)
* Pillkomayo: It probably is the representation of the Sacred River: Vilcanota o Willka Mayu.

UKHU
* The eyes: Imaymana ñauraykunaq ñauin. This could refer to ancestral gods or seeds.

Masculine side
ORQORARA
Feminine side
It probably represented the constellation of Orion, with a meaning that could refer to the "Reunion or Gathering of many Gods" and in short, this would be the panel´s title

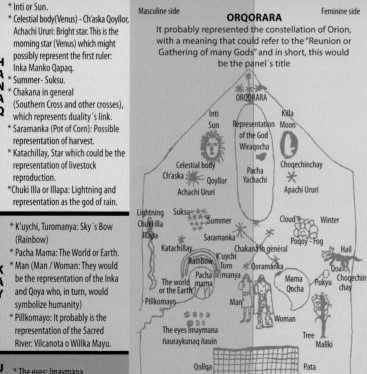

HANAQ
* Killa or Moon.
* Choqechinchay, Apachi Ururi: This is the evening star (Venus) which possibly represented Mama Oqllo, the first Qoya.
* Winter- Poqoy.
* Qoramanka (Pot of herbs) opposite of Saramanka
* Qoa or Choqechinchay: Hail that would be the representation of the luminous feline which foretells hail storms.

KAY
* Pukyu: Springs or water holes which create lagoons.
* Mama Qocha: Mother Sea.
* Woman (Man / Woman: They would be the representation of the Inka and Qoya who, in turn, would symbolize humanity)

UKHU
* The tree, Mallki (Ancestors) which might represent continuity among generations.

Qolqan - pata, warehouse, terraces or the Qorikancha´s representation.

67

Sacred animals

The Andean vision of the cosmos highlighted certain characteristics and qualities worthy of being admired in animals like:

- **The Serpent or Amaru** which is the symbol of water associated to its fertilizing forces. The Snake is identified with the Lightning. It is the luminous serpent that announces the coming of water or Yakumama. It was represented with one or two heads.
- **The Puma or mountain lion** which stands out, representing strength, power, value, and skill. It is the symbol of powerfulness and discretion; attributes that, at times, seem to be linked with the earth, and at others, these are the bridge that unites terrestrial forces with the supernatural world.
- **The Condor or kuntur** was a deity considered as a symbol of wisdom, messenger of the gods, in addition of being the mediator between the three worlds.

Felines were present for thousands of years, and the puma (Mountain lion) stands out among them.

Bicephalous snake
Pucara Culture

The puma (*Puma concolor*) is original of the Americas:

- It lives in areas that go from sea level, to 4,500 m.a.s.l.
- It is carnivorous and can feed on any animal that it is able to capture.
- It is a solitary feline.
- It is a great predator and it very rarely attacks people.

The condor (*Vultur gryphus*)
It belongs to the cathartid family; word that comes from the Greek word kathartes and means "he who cleanses".

- Its habitat is the Andean Cordillera.
- It mainly feeds on carrion.
- It is the world's largest flying bird.
- It is monogamous.
- It builds its nest between 3,000 and 5,000 meters of altitude.
- It has a wingspan of about 3 m. and weighs between 10 and 15 kilos.

Female

Male

People in charge of the cult

The cult and religious offices were entrusted to a numerous group of people; each individual with determined functions. Among them, stood out, the Willaq Uma or Priest of the highest level, who could be the Inka's brother or uncle.

It was very important to maintain a rigorous performance of the religious rituals, so that the numerous gods remained satisfied and willing to provide for and satisfy their people's needs, maintaining harmony in the world.

Ceremonial rites

They were performed with great submission and humility. But, generally, they ended with great joy and presentation of dances accompanied by abundant drink and food.

During the ceremonies and rites, a series of practices were performed, such as:

- The T'inka or offering that denotes a sort of magical communion with the gods.
- Divination mainly performed with coca leaves and organs of sacrificed animals.
- Pilgrimages, fasting, abstinence, etc.
- A variety of offerings, among which the "haywakuy" (To offer) stands out as a very much spread out custom, even in our present days.

The first samples of the cult to the Pachamama were found in Kotosh's Temple, in Huánuco (2000 b.C.).

Ritual products

A variety of products were used to make offerings to the deities, and among them stand out: The mama sara or maize converted in beverage or bread, coca, seashell called spondylus, cameloid fat and amulets (Qonopas or illas).

Ritual corn cobs

Maize (*Zea mays*) was considered as a sacred plant, food of the gods and indispensable for the journey to the world beyond after death.

Currently, this sign is hung nearby the chichería's door, only when there is chicha.

The aqha, better known as chicha, is a homemade fermented beverage, elaborated with germinated corn. It has medicinal, nutritional and energizing properties. Therefore, it is considered as a sacred beverage.

THE COCA LEAVES

The coca (*Erythroxylum coca*) grows in warm and humid areas, between 800 and 2,000 m.a.s.l. It is still considered as magical and sacred. In Inkan times, it was a product for the elite's exclusive consumption and it was very important in the reciprocity system.

Its chewing became generalized during the time period of the Colony.

It has nutritional, stimulating, anaesthetic, therapeutic properties and it mitigates fatigue, hunger and thirst.

The coca leaf contains 18 alkaloids, along with proteins, carbohydrates, vitamins and minerals.

One of these 18 alkaloids is cocaine in its natural state. This alkaloid was discovered in 1850, by Albert Niemann.

The isolated analysis of this alkaloid shows that its separate consumption does not produce the same effect than when it is consumed as a whole (Coca leaf). In addition, when we chew the coca leaf, our digestive system can convert 75% of the cocaine in ecgonina which is a substance with anaesthetic and analgesic properties.

Drugs like cocaine chlorine hydrate, cocaine basic paste or cocaine base, are elaborated with a variety of chemical products and they mainly produce greater effect when ingested through the nose, lungs or by intravenous injection.

When they are whole and showy, the coca leaves are called "k'intu", and, when they are put together in groups of three, they fulfill a fundamental role in the communication and intimate union between the human being and Andean divinities.

The "k'intu" is one of the offerings that most please the gods, and it is the fastest way to benefit from divine favors.

The sea shells or "mullu", like the Spondylus princeps, played a fundamental part in the Andean world. They had great ritual value, and served as offerings, as well as adornments, and probably, as a means for exchange or trade, as well.

Human offerings

Human offerings in Inkan times have been an exceptional religious practice, especially to prevent disasters caused by random natural phenomena, such as volcanic eruptions and the El Niño phenomenon.

Few samples of human offerings were found, among which stands out: The Lady of Ampato or Ice Maiden.

Masks

As is the case in other nations, masks have played a very important role in the exteriorization of beliefs, customs, magic and religion. A mask disguises reality, and for a moment, it gives special attributes and qualities to whoever has it on, and which that individual can take advantage of, in order to recreate a myth, make others laugh, make fun of something or satirize some character, etc.

Cultural manifestations

Their cultural manifestations maintain the spirit and behavior of the Andean people of all times. The Inkas inherited them and were inspired by them, to create their own manifestations, in which prevailed the sense of symmetry and simplicity, with a geometrical tendency.

These manifestations always were influenced by social, political and particularly, religious factors.

They used a broad range of natural resources to get the most varied colors.

Textile work

It was an activity performed on a broad scale. Not only with the purpose of making clothes, but also, because it was part of the reciprocity system and ritual practices.

In the confection of woven fabrics, the wool of South American cameloids was used, as well as cotton and bast. The Inkas used an enormous palette of colors, with which they obtained a most varied quantity of designs. They had a predilection for tapestry work.

Cochineal is an insect from which the ancient Peruvians extracted hues of carmine color, especially for dying woven fabrics.

Feathery art

For their shiny and beautiful colors, their delicate texture and scarcity, feathers were elements with symbolic values and special cultural connotations, destined to dress members of the nobility. Therefore, the Inkas made tufts, umbrelas and fabrics with feathers.

Inkan feather Unku

CLOTHES OF THE INKA AND QOYA

1. Ribbon: Llauto
2. Tassel: Maskaypacha
3. Sceptre: Suntur pawkar
4. Earring: Tulumpi
5. Bracelet: Chipana
6. Cape: Llakolla
7. Tunic: Unku
8. Fringe with designs: Tokapu
9. Fringe work: Saqsa
10. Sandals: Usuta

1. Head dress: Ñañaka
2. Shawl: Lliklla
3. Pin: Tupu
4. Flower: T'ika
5. Waist band: Chumpi
6. Purse: Ch'uspa
7. Tunic: Aksu o kusma
8. Sandals: Usuta

Both wore the best garments elaborated with very fine fibers, like that of the vicuna.

Music and dance

Both manifestations fulfilled a very important part in social, agricultural and religious life, as means of accompaniment in rites and ceremonies, dynamics for work, leisure and entertainment.

The Inkas had several wind and percussion musical instruments, such as quenas, quenachos, antaras, zampoñas, tarkas, sikus, wankar, baqueta, pinkullos, okarinas, pututus, bombos, jingle sticks, rattles, drums, etc.

Dancing was a practice with a magical character. It was executed to give thanks for harvests, venerate divinities, get rid of diseases, etc

(GPA)

The seashell or "pututu" was a sound communication and musical instrument ▶ which had magical and religious connotations, at all times in the Andean culture.

Andean music was executed on the basis of the pentatonic scale.

The Vicus stood out in the manufacturing of objects, with water ▶ based sound systems.

72

Ceramics

Another prestigious artistic expression was manifested through ceramics. These were mainly manufactured for domestic or utilitarian uses, although, the Inkas also elaborated other very fine ceramics for religious purposes. There was a wide variety of shapes and decorative patterns that maintained a standard trend. Chávez Ballón says the most characteristic ones were the "Inkaq P'uyñun" ❶, better known as "aríbalo" (Jars) and the "kero" or ceremonial vessel ❷.

The huacos or portraits present an extraordinary realism. The Mochicas stood out in the fabrication and decoration of ceramics.

Sicán mask

Sculpture

It was one of the first artistic manifestations, and generally, it was performed in stone. In Inkan times, small sculptures stood out, that were used as ritual and ceremonial objects. They were characterized by the simplification of their shapes.

Metallurgy

Gold, silver and copper were used and alloys of tin and copper were developed, to obtain bronze. The Inkas also knew lead and mercury, but they very rarely used them.

They did not know iron.

The metallic art pieces of different sizes, had ornamental purposes and served as offerings to the divinities. Therefore, just as the woven fabrics did, they allowed identifying prestige or status.

Chimú Tumi

Inkan Corn cob made of silver

Bronze was the metal most frequently used for the manufacture of tools, such as chisels, as it was hard and durable.

The best exponents in goldsmith work were the Sicán, and later on, the Chimú.

(A/P)

73

Engineering and architecture

In ancestral Andean society, disciplines and activities formed a whole integrated into nature, respecting and complementing its laws.

The Inkan State's architecture and engineering were activities intensively performed throughout the territory. These were the product of the experience of their predecessors and contemporaries, of perfecting their criteria and pragmatic spirit, as they reached astounding levels, as much in technology, as in the quantity of construction works achieved in less than a century. They managed to achieve the greatest construction works in the ancient Andean world, as a sample and instrument of their power and dominion.

Representative Inkan engineering and architectural works

• Paths

One of the important aspects within the Inkan State's planning was to have administrative centers and a broad road infrastructure of more than thirty thousand kilometers. In that way, the territory was interconnected and unified, and in addition, this gave life to the administration and economic flux, as well as to religious and cultural life.

The "Qapaq Ñan", Main Path or Inka's Path was the State's vertebral spine, the fundamental means of integration and development of the Tawantinsuyo, and the city of Cusco was its central convergence point.

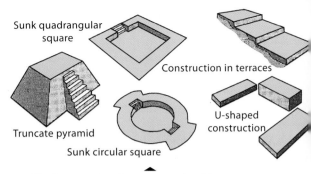

Sunk quadrangular square

Construction in terraces

Truncate pyramid

U-shaped construction

Sunk circular square

The first samples of monumental architecture, as a developed expression, correspond to thousands of years before the Inkas and they were closely related to religion and astronomy.

- - - The Tawantinsuyo's borders
— Longitudinal paths
— Transversal paths
● Cusco
• Inkan settlements

Path signaled with landmarks

Compacted dirt path

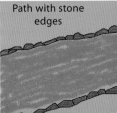

Path with stone edges

These paths were carefully traced, according to topography and functionality, with milestones that indicated distances, and they were provided with bridges and tambos, as well as with stairs, tunnels, pavement, drainage, etc.

There were no means of locomotion with wheels. They did not use the wheel.

• Tambos

These were inns and warehouses at the same time. There were tambos of different categories and sizes, supplied with food, clothes, firewood and weapons. Furthermore, they had pens for animals, and were situated wherever it was necessary.

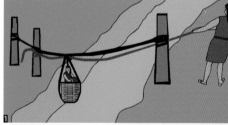

• Bridges

The Inkas built bridges of different kinds. According to needs, these could be hanging, fixed, strategic, of rolled earth, barges on rivers with calm waters, and oroyas **1**.

Chaskis

It was an efficient messenger service system that worked as a post network. It was the key to an efficient administration and control of the Inkan State. Chasquis could deliver a message from Cusco to Lima, in 3 days and from Cusco to Quito, in between 5 and 8 days, considering an average relay run of 250 km. / day.

Q'eswachaka

Last Inkan hanging bridge in use, made with braided "ichhu" (Wild altitude grass), in the way of cables, which allows crossing the Apurimac River ▶ that runs along the bottom of a deep gorge. The reconstruction ritual of this bridge, which is performed every year, is registered as National Cultural Patrimony.

- **Ships**

  The Inkas intensively exploited the sea's resources, using sea faring crafts like the little totora horses, as well as other more sophisticated ones.

  In Pachakuteq's time, his son Tupaq Yupanki made a long expedition to the legendary islands of Awachumbi and Ninachumbi (Oceania).

TUPAQ YUPANKI'S TRANSOCEANIC ADVENTURE

Tupaq Yupanki was the victorious Inka who conquered great part of the Tawantinsuyo's territory and also made the most important maritime journey of Peruvian antiquity.

It is impossible to discard the hypothesis that the 10th Inka, when still a Prince, discovered Oceania (Without knowing it) and also got to the Mangareva Island or Awachumbi and Easter Island or Ninachumbi. That is to say that he crossed the Pacific Ocean in 1465 a.D., 55 years before Hernando de Magallanes.

How did he do it?

- He had unsinkable rafts built with sails, and launched from the equatorial coast (Probably from Manta).
- There might have been 120 ships, with a total crew of 2,000 men.
- He would have crossed the Pacific Ocean in about 90 days (4,000 nautical miles), taking advantage of winds and currents.
- As food stocks, they carried water in canes and gourds, as well as dehydrated food, and took advantage of seafood.

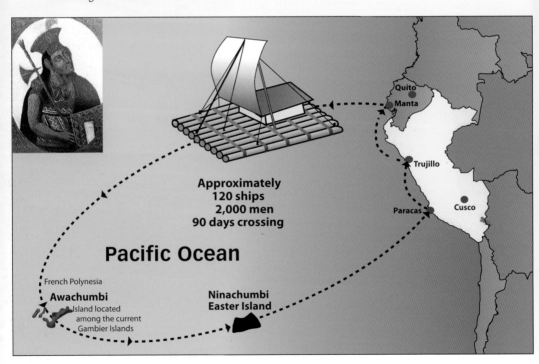

Approximately
120 ships
2,000 men
90 days crossing

Pacific Ocean

French Polynesia
Awachumbi
Island located
among the current
Gambier Islands

**Ninachumbi
Easter Island**

Quito
Manta
Trujillo
Paracas
Cusco

• Temples

Religion played a predominant part in the Tawantinsuyo's political governing process. Therefore, temples and places of cult were true works of art closely related to astronomy. Recording astronomical phenomena, structured Inkan society's activities.

During the Colony, between 1539 and 1650, many campaigns were undertaken to destroy native religious sites and later on, to discover treasures. In spite of it all, there are still beautiful examples in existence.

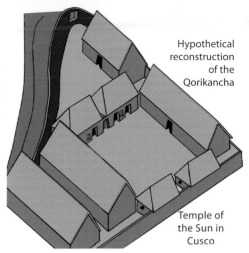

Hypothetical reconstruction of the Qorikancha

Temple of the Sun in Cusco

• Cities (Llaqtas)

The Inkan society was fundamentally agricultural; reason for which it did not propitiate urban development, even during the State's greatest development time period.

Therefore, the specialization of work must have oriented urban development towards the foundation of llaqtas or administrative and religious centers (Centers of political, religious and astronomical power), more than that of cities. From there, decentralized control was being exercised; that is to say, these were social settlements that had the characteristic of being dispersed.

The people's architecture, as it was almost entirely dedicated to agriculture, did not reach levels comparable to that of the State, as the peasants had rustic houses, generally located in the fields they cultivated.

THE CITY OF CUSCO HAD THE SHAPE OF A LYING PUMA

		Inkan Neighborhoods		
Ⓐ Saqsaywaman	Ⓓ Qorikancha	① Qolqanpata ④ Rimaqpampa ⑦ Kayaukachi ⑩ K'illipata
Ⓑ Waqaypata	⬤ Hanan Qosqo	② Qantupata ⑤ Pumaqchupan ⑧ Ch'akillchaka ⑪ Karmenqa
Ⓒ Kusipata	⬤ Hurin Qosqo	③ T'oqokachi ⑥ Qoripata ⑨ Picchu ⑫ Wakapunku

The first known manifestation of urban society on the American continent, was the city of Caral (3000 b.C.).

During colonial times, the population was concentrated in villages called reductions, to control the indigenous dispersion and better use that labor force.

- **Kancha (Housing block)**

  It was the basic and generalized construction pattern for temples, palaces and homes.

  The rooms were arranged around a central patio, and surrounded by a wall, encircling the enclosure, with only one access way.

- **Usnu**

  Structure generally made of stone, situated in the center of the square, upon which the Inka presided ceremonies.

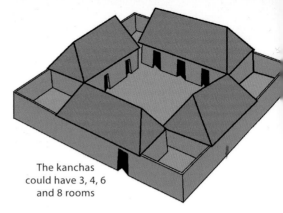

The kanchas could have 3, 4, 6 and 8 rooms

F. Ochoa says that the "Usnu" of the city of Cusco, was a platform with fine walls, situated at the center of the Main Square, where the most important ceremonies were performed. It was the place where the Sun God or "Inti" descended to drink the "chicha" or "aqha" offered in gold vessels.

Building techniques

Inkan architecture and engineering probably were the most important activities, in their eagerness to integrate the numerous ethnic groups that lived in the ancient Andean world.

The Inkas used organization, as well as planning principles and criteria, for the layout, design and execution of their construction works, in close relation with geographical, geomorphic, topographic and hydrological aspects, and all of that, with the aim of achieving harmony and balance between their construction works and nature.

When the conflict between Waskar and Atawallpa broke out, all construction activities were abandoned. Then, during the conquest and colonization process, these were omitted because of neglect, interests for finances or power, etc., substituting them for European style constructions, with new procedures, parameters and concepts, leaving aside ancestral construction techniques and materials.

The existence of so many and such excellent construction works, motivated many professionals to research, decipher and give comprehensible answers, especially regarding the techniques and mechanisms used by the Inkas, although some still keep their secrets.

Building materials

The Inkas especially used stone, such as limestone, diorite, granite, andesite, basalt and others. They also used earth, wood and vegetable fibers.

The "ichhu" (Stipa ichu) or wild straw is a multiple-use graminea that grows in high Andean areas.

"Adobes" or large sun-dried mud bricks, made with ancestral techniques, for the restoration of the Temple of Wiraqocha, in Raqchi.

TYPES OF BUILDING TECHNIQUES

The walls present different types of "aparejo" (This is the way or modality in which materials are being set in a construction), according to the shape, size and location of the stones. Generally, they were related with the function given to the building, but not because of a chronological or civilizations difference.

Some samples of the different types of building materials made with smoothened, cut and worked natural stones, in varied shapes and sizes, that display different joints, profiles, textures and fittings.

The variety of aspects and quality of building materials (Over 20 different types), are a sample of the abundance of imagination the Inkan architects put into their engineering works.

Construction phases of buildings with fine finish

• Extraction of stones

The majority of quarries were located relatively close by or on the construction site and rock falls were taken advantage of.

Then, the stones could be extracted, detached, cut or sectioned, taking advantage of natural fracture lines (Disjunctions), using stones and/or levers (Bronze bars or resistant wood).

Some quite widely spread speculations, to explain the breaking of the rocks:

- One sustains that dry wooden wedges, inserted in the previously opened orifices, in a stone, as they dilate under the action of water, may cause its fracturing.
- Another one says that the stones could be fractured by means of abrupt temperature changes, heating them up with fire, and then, cooling them down with cold water.
- There also is a possible technique that would consist in filling the holes or slits carved into the stone, with water, so that it might freeze during the night, and produce its breaking apart.

▲ It probably was common practice to break or fragment medium size and small stones, with hard and heavy stones, with or without the help of chisels or wedges, whether these might be made of stone or metal.

Stone in the process of being cut or split into two pieces, by percussion, forming a kind of neck or groove. J. P. Protzen asserts that it probably was the most frequently used technique, to separate large stone blocks.

Protzen says that, in order to drag a stone, the number of men needed to do so, was evaluated in relation to its size, as well as to the characteristics of the itinerary to be covered.
It is possible that they might have dragged the rock, using a sort of net made of resistant ropes, while other men pushed from behind it, using levers.

Another probable carrying technique was that of using two overlapping ladders, as the lower one was stuck to the ground by gravity, and the stone block was attached to the upper one which worked like a sled, moving ▼ along, under the impulse of levers.

• Transportation

For larger stones, the Inkas took advantage of cliffs and natural slides, as well as of ramps and inclined slopes they built, to slide them, and in other cases, they would take advantage of soft slopes, perhaps covered with pebbles, fine sand and clay, to haul them.

They also used wooden rolls and stone cylinders or balls called qollotas, as well as levers, to push and lift.

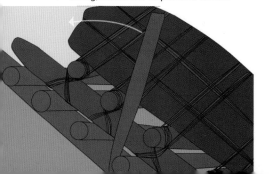

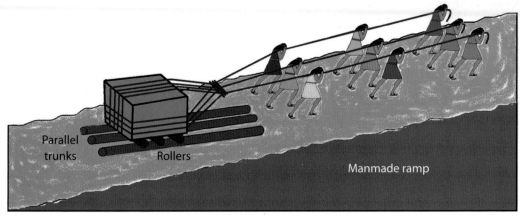

Parallel trunks

Rollers

Manmade ramp

The small stones were carried by men, with or without the help of ropes, and for the medium size ones, they used a stretcher-like device, made of large wooden poles.

- **Stone carving**

  The stones were carried to the work place, where they were generally carved in the planned shape and size. To do so, the main percussion technique was used, with hard stone hammers which had mechanical characteristics of resistance and elasticity, like rounded edges, and were made of pure quartzite, granite, basalt, hematite, etc., with different sizes and weights, according to the carving phases, and weighed from less than 1 kilo, to over 10 kilos. J.P. Protzen says: "The heaviest ones were used to break larger stones into smaller blocks, the medium size ones, to carve the sides or faces and the small ones, to carve the edges and angles".

Spherical percussion tools

"Small stone hammers were used to carve the edges and angles."

The Inkas knew the direction of the diaclase in stones, and used stones, as well as bronze chisels, to smoothen and cut them.

"They used medium-size stone hammers, to cut and give the finishing touches on the sides or faces of the stone blocks."

For each phase of the building process, the techniques and tools were used in function of available materials and their characteristics, as well as the architectural style and dexterity of the labor force.

These techniques were perfected through generations, with dedication and patience.

"Female" hiwaya (Hematite)

Compact sedimentary rocks, much harder than that which is carved (They contain 70% iron oxide). Male and female "hiwaya" stones.

"Male" hiwaya (Hematite)

Planed down faces, both of which had to be carved, as part of the inlaying process, until the final settling of the stone was managed through the "trial and error" technique.

The stones used in the foundations and laying of fine finish walls, display slightly concave and convex faces, in helicoidal planes, to ensure a perfect fit and a good resistance.

Stones inlaid with admirable precision. ▼

- **Inlay, seating and operation of stones**

Without a doubt, this is the most astounding feature of fine finish constructions, since between stone and stone, there is no space left at all.

They used the following techniques:
- Friction of one stone against another.
- "Trial and error": Technique by means of which the stones were set in their planned space and then, removed, to retouch them and readjust their inlay. Constant practice and specialization made it so that, each time, the number of trials and errors decreased.
- They probably used sorts of models or patterns and molds, by means of which the stones were previously cut, to have them fit in the planned place.
- The combination of the previous ones.

◀ Stone in a destroyed wall in which one can observe the way the stones were carved, and upon which the following layers of stones were inlaid and seated.

In the stones' perfect fitting of a wall, the lines and right angles are apparent.

Each stone is a resistant structural element, and is conveniently fitted with the others which act and react, under the effects of the different types of loads or external forces.

They managed to unite stones with such exactitude that, in some cases, it is almost impossible to perceive the line that separates one stone from the next.

There are stones with different kinds of carved slits used to maintain the stones united one with the other, by means of copper or bronze clamps, although no such Inkan clamps have been found.

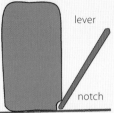
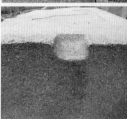

In the same way as the protuberances of different shapes and dimensions, the notches and grooves were used for the manipulation of the stones.

lever

notch

They were used to move them by means of levers or ropes, as well as to mark and make their carving easier, or as support points, to maintain them in a tilted position, etc.

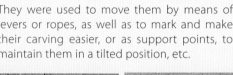

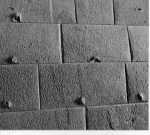

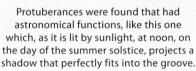

▲ Like this protuberance, many of these have been destroyed.

◄ Protuberances that probably served as decorative and ideographic elements…

Generally, the finishing work on the external faces was done once the stone was set ▼ in its final place.

Protuberances were found that had astronomical functions, like this one which, as it is lit by sunlight, at noon, on the day of the summer solstice, projects a shadow that perfectly fits into the groove. ▼

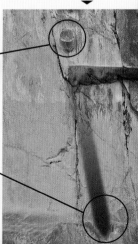

Destroyed walls that show different inner structures.

They used bedrocks as foundations, carving concave cavities into them.

- **Polish**

  It was part of the finishing work and was done by means of friction with dirt and water or humidified sand (Quartz silicate sand).

Some building details

- **The foundations**

  Depending on the kind of terrain and construction, the foundations were raised, with special care for the drainage system. Generally, small stones were stacked without digging a ditch, and fitted together with or without mud mortar.

- **The walls**

  For the erection of walls, they used embankments or slanted surfaces, and probably, scaffoldings.

Structures perfectly made in the adequate shape, dimension, position, relation, etc., to resist the consequences of the action of loads and external forces.

Precise calculations on the materials' own resistance, as well as on their resistance and elasticity properties, induce us to affirm that Inkan architecture has the "S" of Solidity, Symmetry, Simplicity and Safety.

In general, Inkan walls presented a slight inclination towards the inside; a quality that gives them greater stability and solidity, during earthquakes.

(GPA)

AMOIOMADORESDESTEREINO.
VVACAVCHO COMARAQVI
INGA   INGA

- **The stone nails**

  Inside the enclosures, there are still stone nails which were used as furniture, in the same way the niches were, and also served as hangers, for all kinds of ritual and domestic objects.

- **The niches**

  Inkan buildings present niches on their inside, which were used as altars, and to keep ritual or domestic objects.

  The external niches might have been ornamental and possibly, in the same way as some entrance ways and windows, they might have allowed some kind of interpretation, due to the contrast of light and shadow they created.

- **The windows**

  In general, the windows in Inkan buildings are small and have a ventilation function, more than that of illuminating.

- **The entrance ways**

  The access ways, windows and niches have a trapezoidal shape, in the same way as the buildings do. The entrance ways can be with simple or double jambs and exceptionally, with triple jamb.

  Those with double or triple jamb indicate the enclosure's importance, along with the entrance ways that have a restrictive access system.

The entrances had no doors. Instead, they were equipped with a system to restrict access or to indicate the absence of the inhabitant, which consisted in a crossbar or crossing rope, or also, in two poles in the shape of a "+". These elements were attached with a rope to a ring located on the lintel and in the lateral notches, in the inner part of the entrances.

- **Plasters**

  The buildings made of rustic materials (Stone and sun-dried mud bricks), and exceptionally, the fine finishing touches, were covered and coated with high quality clay, and many were even painted.

  The majority of Inkan constructions were of a rustic type, made with rough or semi-carved stones and sun-dried mud bricks (Adobes).

◄ The trapezoidal shape is an unmistakable characteristic of inkan architecture.

◄ Construction in stone and sun-dried mud bricks (Adobes): Samples of efficiency, when combining the available resources.

- **The floors**

  Generally, they were of compacted clay and soil placed on a layer of pebbles. However, the Inkas also used stones.

Almost all constructions that are identified as Inkan today, pertain to activities performed after 1440.

- **The roofs**

  They built roofs with 1, 2 and 4 slopes, as well as in conic shapes, which had a wooden frame and a waterproof layer of straw, of almost 50 cm. in thickness, with a durability of over 5 years.

Stone pegs and flat stones, with holes were used to tie the roof down and secure it.

Inner structure of the ceiling ▼

THE SPANISH CONQUEST

Some decisive factors for the conquest were the following:

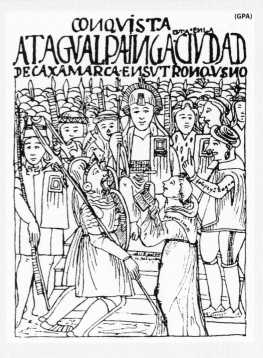

- Atahuallpa knew about the conquerors' arrival on the Tahuantinsuyo's coasts. But, his curiosity and excessive self-confidence prevented him to perceive their technological superiority or war strategies, and instead of blocking their progression, he eased their way in, and with their first encounter, he put an end to Inkan sovereignty.
- The Spanish took advantage of and handled with much skill the conjuncture of a State destabilized by civil war and the irreversible division between the panakas (Royal families) of the aspirants to the throne: Wascar and Atawallpa.
- Some ethnic groups conquered by the Inkas, took advantage of the Spaniards' arrival, and joined them, in the aim of recuperating their autonomy. Therefore, this fact shows that the populations' integration within the Tawantinsuyo, still had a long way to go.
Besides, the Inkan power's supremacy was far from being consolidated.
- The Spanish aroused past conflicts among Andean inhabitants and introduced new intrigues.
- The diffusion of unknown diseases which devastated the native populations, before and after the conquest (Since the decade of 1520).
- Many of the conquerors had greater experience in warfare.
- They meticulously studied and planned their war strategies, in accordance with the Andean people's idiosyncrasy and existing circumstances.
- Violence and cruelty were established, maintaining the Andean people in constant uncertainty between collaboration and resistance.

THE COLONIAL PHASE

The colonial phase that lasted almost three centuries of excessive contrarieties, conflicts and drastic changes that caused serious collective impact on a psychological and emotional level (Although there also were development and material progress), slowly and paradoxically shaped a multi-cultural and multi-ethnical Peru which, with its political independence from Spain, between 1821 and 1824, managed a Republic which was not very different from the Colony, especially in social aspects.

So, Peru's Republican life went on 'till a few decades ago, without taking advantage of the opportunities granted by democracy, such as equality and freedom, which Peru still lacks, and therefore, still has to face challenges which, on the basis of past mistakes and successes, are designing an appropriate development, in order to forge an independent and prospering society.

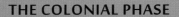

The weapons the conquerors used (For example, the muskets and crossbows), had an effect 50 times superior to that of Andean weapons. In addition, their efficiency was being quadrupled as they were used by soldiers mounted on horses and dressed in armor.

SOME ANDEAN WEAPONS

Mass

Maqana

▲The "estólica" or dart propeller was the weapon most feared by the conquerors.

Spear

Sling

Shield

Porra

Hatchets

SOME SPANISH WEAPONS

Crossbow

Musket

Cavalry

Cannon

PERU'S TOURIST ATTRACTIONS

(MTa)

(WH)

Imagine yourself, awakening at the foot of the Andes, to breathe the purest air and feel the morning breeze, while you see the Sun rise and walk out to contemplate the most beautiful landscapes that surrender at your feet. Later on, take a sun bath on the beach, enjoy fresh fish, hear the sea's pleasant waves and feel delighted by the imposing sky's colors. The Sun is going down. At night, you go to enjoy one of the most varied culinary traditions; products of countless cultural blends gifted with the most diverse flavors and colors, and appreciate other cultural expressions manifested through art. Be a part of a unique culture, meanwhile you observe the most varied dances, costumes, masks, etc.

Imagine yourself, awakening on a Lake Titicaca island, surrounded by the water's intense blue which fuses with the sky's radiant light blue and the nearby Sun… You have the sensation that you could caress the sky. Now, you understand why the Inkas called it "The Origin of the Cosmos".

You've just gotten in touch with nature, as you had never done it before. You have seen all sorts of animals, superb gigantic trees which have been witnesses of history, the most impressive colors of flowers, and tasted exotic flavors of the Peruvian jungle's fruit. Then, you navigate on a canoe, on the river, and can still hear the animals' celebration, in the jungle. The Sun is hiding in the distance, and still, you cannot believe how wonderful everything that surrounds you is.

Imagine yourself, awakening and feeling the energy of one of the most imposing Inkan architectural achievements: Machupicchu. It is a master blend of human genius and respect towards nature's harmonic beauty… in perfect balance, with both parts cohabitating in harmony and accepting each other. You can already feel the magic, while you go through that colorful jungle and feel evermore enthusiastic and ready to face new challenges.

Back in Cusco, you wander about the streets and appreciate Inkan walls that blend with the colonial past, giving you the sensation of being in another time frame. Now, you are getting lost in the star spangled night and feel happy about having enjoyed one of the world's most wonderful places.

Andrea González N.

Peru has a broad range of attractions offered in different visit and activity alternatives, for all kinds of public, along with beautiful sceneries full of cultural and natural wealth, to delight the most demanding visitor.

Be a part of this wonder!

Main Square (MTa)

Colonial windows (MTa)

(DS) 1

TRUJILLO (34 m.a.s.l.)

City of the Eternal Spring				
Climate		From Lima	Population	
Warm	Temp.	Max. 26°C	By plane: 50 min.	2011: 899,709	Inhab.
		Min. 14°C	By car: 8 h.	2015: 957,010	

Trujillo is the capital city of the Department of La Libertad. That city displays beautiful samples of colonial and republican architecture, to which are summed up archaeological complexes, among which Chan Chan is the world's largest mud brick city.

The Northern Marinera 1

The Marinera is considered as Peru's National Dance, and among its different versions, the Northern Marinera stands out.

The National Northern Marinera Contest takes place in the city of Trujillo, during the last week of January of each year.

Peruvian Step Horses 2

(DS) 2
(MTa) 3

Race of horses improved over more than 300 years, after their arrival in Peru.

Enjoy the dance performed by these beautiful step horses, in Trujillo.

Huanchaco

It is a seaside resort where one can appreciate the "caballitos de totora"3 which are sea faring crafts that, in the past, were used for fishing.

Huanchaco Resort (MTa)

(WS) **1** **2**

Decorated frieze with the image of the Moche God, Ai Apaec or throat cutting divinity.

Chan Chan

Chan Chan's archaeological area is Humanity's Cultural Patrimony, as it was declared as such by the UNESCO, in 1986.

Chan Chan **1** was the Chimú culture's most important city. It was built in three stages and is composed of monumental buildings and marginal neighborhoods, which shows a clear social class stratification. Its beautiful walls decorated in high-relief call the visitors' attention.

Huacas of the Sun and Moon

One had an administrative purpose (Huaca of the Sun) and the other, religious purposes (Huaca of the Moon **2**), as they were constructions in which millions of sun-dried mud bricks were used.

The El Brujo Archeological Complex

The Huaca of Cao Viejo is located in this complex, where the tomb of a Sovereign, the Lady of Cao, was discovered.

THE LADY OF CAO

In 2005, in the Archaeological Complex of El Brujo (Trujillo), the mummified body of a woman was found, in excellent state of conservation (Thanks to the cinnabar or mercury sulphate), and who was given the name of "The Lady of Cao".

Who was the Lady of Cao?

- She was one of the Mochica culture's rulers (Chicama Valley), about 1,700 years ago (4th century a.D.).
- She was not buried alone, and was given the funerary dowry which presents a variety of rich objects. It is deduced that she had a high leader status, with magical and religious powers, a semi-divine condition and gifts as a prophet.
- One of the details that most call one's attention, are the snake and spider tattoos of mystical character, designed on her skin.
- She passed away between 20 and 25 years of age.
- She was 1.45 m. tall.
- In spite of her apparent fragility, she did not suffer from nutritional deficiencies or development problems.
- She displays very good health conditions.

91

CHICLAYO (46 m.a.s.l.)

Climate		From Lima	Population	
It is mild and dry, due to the presence of winds	Temp.	Max. 30°C / By plane: 1 h.	2011: 829,051	Inhab.
		Min.15°C / By car: 12 h.	2015: 857,405	

◀ Ear pendant representing the Lord of Sipan

Chiclayo is the capital city of the Department of Lambayeque. There, it is possible to remember the existence of great and powerful leaders of Peru's history, such as the Lord of Sipan. Without a doubt, the burial of that noble gentleman must have been the most pompous in South America.

Túcume

The Architectural Complex of Túcume was the capital city of the Lambayeque culture. It is known as the "Pyramids' Valley", because of the existence of 26 truncated pyramids built with sun-dried mud bricks (Adobes).

Emblem with open arms

THE LORD OF SIPAN

In 1987, in the pre-Inkan archaeological complex of Huaca Rajada, in Sipan which is located in Chiclayo — Lambayeque and pertained to the Mochica culture, the Royal Tombs of Sipan were discovered, among which stands out that of the Lord of Sipan; the first in its kind that was discovered in America.

Who was the Lord of Sipan?

• He was a Mochica ruler who lived around 250 a.D.

• Possibly, this political, military and religious chief died because of a disease or an epidemic, at the approximate age of 40.

• He was 1.67 m. tall.

• He was healthy, with exception of an incipient arthritis.

• He had a body structure with little muscular development, a flattened skull, teeth in good shape, with little wearing away and the Rh negative type of blood (Little common kind of blood).

Kayak on Lindo lake

TARAPOTO (333 m.a.s.l.)

Climate			From Lima	Population	
Warm and humid, with frequent rainfalls	Temp.	Max. 34°C	By plane: 1 h. 10 min.	2011: 71,973	Inhab.
		Min. 19°C	By car: 25 h.	2015: 73,015	

Tarapoto is a city which is located in the Department of San Martín. It is located in the Blue Cordillera which gives way to the Amazonian Basin.

It is known as the land of lagoons **1** and cataracts. In addition, nature's set of shapes and colors, makes it so that any visitor wants to remain there, in ecstasy.

One of the most important cultural attractions is the archaeological complex of the Gran Pajatén which is part of the 36 archaeological sites in the Abiseo River National Park, declared as "Humanity's Cultural and Natural Patrimony" by the UNESCO, in1990.

CHACHAPOYAS (2,334 m.a.s.l.)

Climate			From Lima	Population	
Warm and humid, with rainfalls between the months of November and April	Temp.	Max. 21°C	By car: 21 h.	2011: 54,593	Inhab.
		Min. 9°C		2015: 55,201	

It is the capital city of the Department of Amazonas. The city of Chachapoyas is the departure point for a magical adventure in which one can visit many attractions, among which stand out Kuélap's Fortress **2 5**, as well as the mausoleums and sarcophagus **3** set on impressive cliffs.

Likewise, it is possible to visit the Gocta Cataract **4** which, with its 771 meters, is the third highest in the world.

Otorongo   Macaw

IQUITOS (104 m.a.s.l.)

Climate			From Lima	Population	
Warm and humid, with considerable rainfalls	Temp.	Max. 32°C	By plane: 1 h. 45 min.	2011: 545,095	Inhab.
		Min. 21°C		2015: 563,249	

Iquitos is the capital city of the Department of Loreto. It is situated on the banks of the Amazon River, and is the largest city in Peru's Amazonian region, which one can get to by plane or boat.

Iquitos is the starting point to discovering the Amazonian jungle and enjoying nature's richness in flora and fauna, especially in the National Reserves of Pacaya Samiria and Allpahuayo Mishana.

PUERTO MALDONADO (186 m.a.s.l.)

Climate			From Cusco	Population	
Warm and humid	Temp.	Max. 32°C	By plane: 25 min.	2011: 69,565	Inhab.
		Min. 17°C	By car: 8 h.	2015: 78,378	

Puerto Maldonado is the capital city of the Department of Madre de Dios, also known as the "Capital City of Peru's Biodiversity".

It is the starting point to journey across the planet's most beautiful and enigmatic places which are the zealous guardians of an exuberant flora and fauna, and protectors of native ethnic groups, such as the Piros, Huarayos, Machiguengas, etc.

Here are the Manu and Bahuaja Sonene National Parks, as well as the Tambopata National Reserve waiting for you.

Black caiman   (AB)

Tucaneta

MANU NATIONAL PARK
AND BIOSPHERE RESERVE

t is one of the most astounding natural treasures in Peru and the world. It is unique in its kind, because it shelters three very different ecosystems: Puna (Highlands), cloud forest and low jungle. Therefore, the Manu was declared as "Humanity's Natural Patrimony" and "Biosphere Reserve" by the UNESCO, in 1987.

Going to the Manu is an exciting experience which starts in the city of Cusco. It is recommended to do it during the dry season, and in small groups.

Taricaya turtle

t is a place to experience the most uncommon and intense sensations, as it generates a bit of uneasiness. But, in compensation, it greatly stimulates fantasy and an irresistible sensation of freedom.

There, there are moments of unexplainable loneliness, of unfathomable sounds, overwhelming silence, enchantment, with iridescent colors, of stillness or light movements, freshness and heat, to see what is visible, and at the same time, simply imagine what is hidden and perceive the intangible.

The Manu offers extraordinary and colorful landscapes, as well as new sounds and impacting shapes, mountains, precipices, canyons, high hills, rivers, meanders, marshlands, beaches, swamps, lagoons, lakes, etc., and all of that is propitiated by an abundant wildlife, in bounteous vegetation, with dwarf, cloud and magnificent forests, trees the branches of which are profusely covered with epiphyte plants, lichens, mosses, ferns and orchids, in an exuberance of flowers and much more..

Macaw

(JA)

In the Manu, the fecund animal life is impressive, as it is a paradise for birds (There are hundreds of species), primates, mammals, reptiles, fish, insects, etc.

t is an extraordinary territory which covers 1,881,200 hectares and serves as refuge to a huge variety of plant and animal species.

Humanity should assume better its task and obligation to preserve this so rich natural environment.

Coliespina hummingbird

Llanganuco Lagoon (MTa)

Snow-capped Mount Huascaran (CS)

▼ Mountain biking in the Callejón de Huaylas

(PO)

▼ Inlaid stone head in Chavin de Huantar

(MM)

▼ Chavin de Huantar

(MM)

HUARAZ (3,091 m.a.s.l.)

Climate			From Lima	Population	
Warm and dry	Temp.	Max. 25°C	By plane: 50 min.	2011: 159,125	Inhab.
		Min. 4°C	By car: 8 h.	2015: 166,625	

There are two seasons a year:
The dry season between April and October, and
the rain season between November and March.

Huaraz is the capital city of the Department of Ancash and is located in the central part of the Callejón de Huaylas which is between the White and Black Cordilleras.

It is another one of these fascinating places in Peru.

The Callejón de Huaylas is a valley bathed by the Santa River, where is the Huascaran National Park, declared as "Humanity's Natural Patrimony" by the UNESCO, in 1985. It offers a great variety of impressive landscapes composed of spectacular snow-capped mountains, torrents, lagoons and gorges. There, one can practice a series of activities, such as mountain climbing, cycling, rafting, hiking, etc.

Likewise, there is the Archaeological Complex of Chavin de Huantar, declared as "Humanity's Cultural Patrimony" by the UNESCO, in 1985, with its temple and imposing structure, squares, underground passages, etc. This place of worship is one of pre-Hispanic Peru's best architectural examples.

◀ Quadrangular area connected with the Main Temple which contains impressive passages and galleries.

Main Square (Plaza de Armas) **(MTa)**

LIMA (154 m.a.s.l.)

Climate		Population	
It is mild and has two main seasons a year. Summer, from October to April, with sunny days. Winter, from May to September, with greyish days and lots of humidity	Temp.	Max. 27°C Min.15°C	2011: 9,303,788 2015: 9,904,727	Inhab.

Lima's Historical Center has been declared as Humanity's Cultural Patrimony, by the UNESCO, in 1991.

In the Department of Lima, ten thousand year old remains of the Andean people were found and from that time on, several occupation and progress periods followed, up to the Spanish conquerors' arrival.

The city of Lima was founded on January 18, 1535, by the Spanish conqueror Francisco Pizarro who gave it the name of City of Kings and it was the capital city of South America's Spanish Vice-Royalty, during 300 years.

In the same way, Peru's republican life started in that city, with the proclamation of Independence, on July 28, 1821, by General Don José de San Martín.

Today, it is Peru's capital city and constitutes the country's main center of economic and financial activities, as well as that of services and manufacture, which concentrates more than 50% of the country's industry. It is the city in which one finds the most luxurious residential areas, in contrast with areas among the most depressed and subject to extreme poverty.

Cathedral of Lima ▯

It was built in 1535 and is dedicated to Our Lady of Assumption.

Between 1564 and 1605, the master builder Alonso Beltrán directed its reconstruction in the style of the Cathedral of Seville and in spite of the many changes made in the following 463 years, the Cathedral still conserves its colonial composition and façade.

The Jorge Chávez International Airport is the first entrance gate to the country. Therefore, the city of Lima serves as a link by air and land, with the majority of Peru's attractions.

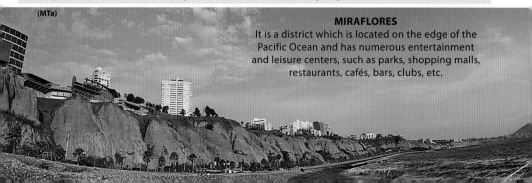

(MTa)

MIRAFLORES
It is a district which is located on the edge of the Pacific Ocean and has numerous entertainment and leisure centers, such as parks, shopping malls, restaurants, cafés, bars, clubs, etc.

(MT)

THE SACRED CITY OF CARAL (3000 to 1800 b.C.)

The Sacred city of Caral – Supe has been declared as Humanity's Cultural Patrimony, by the UNESCO, in 2009, as a property of "exceptional universal value".

Caral, along with Mesopotamia, Egypt, India, China and Central America was one of the original centers of culture, in the world. After its discovery, Peruvian history's chronology had to be rearranged and today, it is considered as the cradle and base of the Andean civilization. In the same way, it is the Americas' oldest known city.

Five thousand years ago, that city was the symbol and capital city of a central government, from which its contemporaneous nations' lives were organized and directed. It was the axis of a broad trading network of products from the coast, mountains and jungle, in an activity developed in a completely peaceful manner, during almost 1,000 years. No remains of weapons were found, nor evidence of any military organization, which caused great surprise among researchers.

(WS) 1

Pachacamac 1

It was one of the Peruvian coast's most important pilgrimage centers. In addition, it was the place from which religious, political and economic decisions were made, during a long time period.

The Inkas respected and venerated that sanctuary. However, they added other buildings, such as the Temple of the Sun and Aklla Wasi or House of the Chosen Women.

(CS) 2

Lachay's Hills 2

It is a National Reserve which shelters one of the world's most original ecosystems. It presents an extraordinary landscape and abundant natural life, in the middle of the desert, thanks to the winter morning fog brought on by trade winds, from the Pacific Ocean.

98

Flamingos in Paracas (CS)

ICA (406 m.a.s.l.)

Climate			From Lima	Population	
Warm and dry all year long	Temp.	Max. 28°C	By car Ica: 4 h. Nazca: 6 h.	2011: 344,430	Inhab.
		Min. 13°C		2015: 362,693	

During the summer months,
the presence of strong winds or paracas is common.

Nine thousand years ago, in today's Santo Domingo de Paracas, Department of Ica, there were human groups considered as the first vegetable garden farmers on the continent. With the passing of time, they forged astonishing civilizations such as:

- **Paracas:** They performed pompous burials, cranial trepanations and unmatchable elaborated textiles.

- **Nazca:** They stood out for their designs on the Nazca and San José plains, as well as for their advanced knowledge in hydraulic engineering, thanks to which they built aqueducts and underground canals that allowed them to develop agriculture in the desert.

- **Chincha:** They were expert fishermen and tradesmen, as they had a great fleet of rafts.

The city of Ica was founded by the Spanish, in 1563, as Villa Valverde, and later on, it was given the denomination of San Jerónimo de Ica. Since the time of the colony, it is a very important wine producing center, and in present days, it is one of the most developed regions in agro-industry, agro-exportation and in the offer of tourist services.

The Huacachina Oasis

This gift from nature is bordered by great sand dunes which invite visitors to the practice of "sandboarding" (Surfing on sand).

The Paracas National Reserve

It is a rich coastal ecosystem composed of deserts, beaches and cliffs. These coastal waters are among the richest in the world, due to the plankton soup found in them.

The Ballestas Islands

These are remains of a coastal mountain range, in which the erosion of the wind and sea has generated classical arches and capricious formations in the rocks, thus creating an impressive landscape.

Paracas Cape (A/P)

(WH)

Paracas' Candlestick (WL)

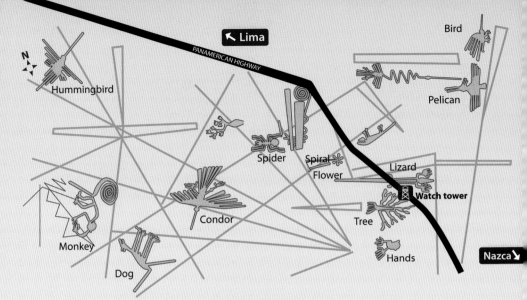

THE NAZCA LINES

The lines and designs of Nazca and Pampas de Jumana are Humanity's Cultural Patrimony, declared by the UNESCO, in 1994.

María Reiche spent her life studying these enigmatic, gigantic and very creative lines which might have been drawn between 300 and 900 a.D, in one of the planet's most arid areas, where it almost never rains (3 mm. every two years).

How were these lines drawn and why did they resist the passing of time?

These designs that display diverse plant, animal and anthropomorphic shapes, are furrows that are only 30 cm. deep, and which are protected by little stones.

The ancient Peruvians made them, drawing aside the reddish superficial ground layer and the following light white sand layer, in which they placed small stones.

The natural gypsum contained in the sand, becomes humid with the dew, which makes it so that the stones remain stuck to the ground. Likewise, as these are exposed to high temperatures during the day, they accumulate heat and create a hot air pillow that isolates the surface, protecting them from the wind and sand.

Which was their function?

It is the most frequently asked question which it is very difficult to give a full answer to.

The meaning of these lines is still being researched. Meanwhile, several hypothesis have been postulated, and the most accepted ones are:

- Around 30% of the drawings have an astronomical relation. Thus, it could be a calendar, in which the shapes might reproduce constellations, and the lines, represent the trajectory of the Sun, Moon and stars, marking solstices, equinoxes and other astronomical events
- Some drawings coincide with underground water layers; reason for which it could be a temple to worship water; a so scarce element in that place, which causes so much concern.
- It might have been a sacred place of pilgrimage or a display for the return of gods who left the terrestrial environment, with the promise to come back.

Yanahuara's vantage point

AREQUIPA (2,350 m.a.s.l.)

Climate			From Lima	Population	
Mild, with moderate rainfalls, from December to March	Temp.	Max. 24°C	By plane: 1 h. 25 min. By car: 15 h.	2011: 925,667	Inhab.
		Min. 6°C		2015: 969,284	

The Historical Center of the city of Arequipa has been declared as Humanity's Cultural Patrimony by the UNESCO, in 2000.

This city is located at the foot of the Misti (Volcano) and in the Chili River Valley; a place which was occupied by some indigenous communities.

That city is known as the "White City", because the use of white volcanic stone predominates in its colonial constructions.

Company of Jesus Church

It shelters true architectural jewels of the Colonial and Republican periods.

In the city, colonial mansions stand out, as well as churches and particularly, the Santa Catalina Convent ❶.

The Colca Canyon

It is one of the deepest canyons on the planet. In addition, it offers a singular natural beauty, punctuated by pre-Hispanic benched terraces that are still cultivated ❷.

Rafting in the Colca Canyon / (A/P)

It also is the place where one can contemplate the flight of the world's largest flying bird: The Condor.

After its magical, spectacular and unforgettable flight, it glides away over long distances, at more than 50 km/h and up to 6.500 m.a.s.l.

Ascent and Sipia Cataracts in Cotahuasi ▶

(PO)

(HP)

❷

THE LADY OF AMPATO OR ICE MAIDEN

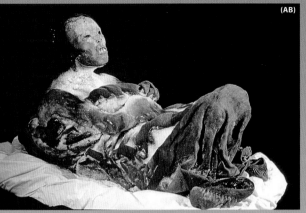

(AB) It is a complete and frozen human body, discovered by John Reinhard (Reason for which it was given the nickname of "Juanita") and Miguel Zárate, in 1995.

Who was the Lady of Ampato?

She was an adolescent chosen and offered to the Apus or mountain divinities, and especially to the Sabancaya volcano.

According to a virtual autopsy performed at the John Hopkins Hospital in Baltimore, Maryland, United States, it is said that Juanita:

(AB)
- Was a maiden of about 14 years of age.
- Was in perfect health and nutritional state.
- There is no evidence of any illness.
- Had strong bones and perfect teeth.

When did she die?

She passed away between 1440 and 1450 a.D., during Inka Pachacutec's government.

How did she die?

She instantaneously died from a blow on the right temple, with a stone club, after having been sedated with aqha or fermented corn beverage. The blow produced a 5 cm. crack and internal hemorrhage.

◀ The girl of Ampato
Gold Illa that represents the Sun. It is one of the three ritual dolls found in the tomb.

Where did they find her?

They found her near the crater of the snow-capped Ampato (6,380 m.a.s.l.), in Arequipa – Peru.

What does Juanita's DNA (Deoxyribonucleic Acid) identification reveal?

In accordance with the genetic world map, she was related with the ancient races original from Taiwan and Korea and in America, with the Ngoge tribe of Panama.

2 Korea
•1 Taiwan
3 Panama
4
Arequipa
Peru

PUNO (3,800 m.a.s.l.)

	Climate		From Cusco	Population	
It's cold and dry	Temp.	Max. 16°C	By plane: 25 min.	2011: 243,441	Inhab.
		Min. -2°C	By car: 7 h.	2015: 248,377	

There are two distinct seasons during the year, which are:
The dry and rainy seasons.
During the rainy season, snow and hail are frequent.

The high plateau has been the scene of the passing of several human groups, among which civilizations like Pukará and Tiawanaco stood out.

Afterwards, several local ethnic groups appeared, among which the Qolla and Aymara stood out, which were conquered by the Inkas and thus, formed one of the Tawantinsuyo's four regions, under the denomination of Qollasuyo; a very important livestock raising area.

Inkan Chullpa

In colonial times, the Laycacota silver ore deposits were discovered, which motivated the foundation of the first Spanish settlement on Lake Titicaca's banks, which was founded in 1668, with the name of Villa San Carlos de Austria.

Finally, in 1805, it was granted the category of city, with the name of Puno.

The Department of Puno has the livestock raising activity as its main economic source, since it is the first producer of South American cameloids, meanwhile the city of Puno is dedicated to commerce, as well as to tourist activities.

Qolla Chullpa

Sillustani

These are pre-Hispanic remains which are located on the banks of Lake Umayo. They were funerary constructions; cylindrical towers called chullpas, from the pre-Inkan and Inkan periods, among which the ones with fine finish, made by the Inkas, stand out.

There are about 90 chullpas to which are added the semi buried underground and underground tombs which are disseminated on an area of 150 hectares.

Stone sculpture in Sillustani ▶
which looks like a puma's head.

Festivity of the Candlemas Virgin or "Mamacha Candelaria" in Puno

It is the most important festivity in the Department of Puno, celebrated between January 24 and February 18 of each year, in a colorful parade, with music and dances, as a display of faith and gratefulness for that Virgin who represents the Pachamama or Mother Earth.

Lake Titicaca

It is the remainder of an older lake known as Ballivián that had a much greater extension, as is evidenced by the terraces with lake-side deposits located over 100 m. above the present water level.

During the last 11 thousand years, the Titicaca was down to 50 m. lower than the present water level, and later on, the connection between the major and minor lakes was re-established. In the same way, between the last 2,000 and 1,000 years, the lake took its present shape and its effluent, the Desagüadero was formed, which evacuates about 5% of the lake's water towards Lake Poopó. However, the Titicaca loses the majority of its waters through evaporation, as a consequence of the high luminous intensity, low temperatures and dry air.

The lake fulfills the function of stabilizing or moderating the temperature of the surrounding areas, making them less cold than the rest of the Collao high plateau, as the heat retained by its waters during the day, is released during the night.

Taquile

Taquile Island is recognized for the textile art elaborated by its inhabitants, with ancestral techniques. It was declared as Humanity's Immaterial Cultural Patrimony by the UNESCO, in 2008.

It is the world's highest navigable lake.

The lake's most important tributaries are the Huancané, Ilave, Coata Ramis and Suches.

Altitude: 3,810 m.a.s.l.	
Total area: 8,562 km².	
Peruvian Sector: 4,996 km² (59.6%)	
Length: 179 km.	
Breadth: 65 km.	
Maximum depth: 281 m.	
Average Annual Temperature: 10°C	
Straight of Tiquina: 600 m.	
Transparency: From 15 to 65 m.	

Lake Titicaca is the Department of Puno's most important tourist attraction.

The Andean populations believed that the Sun and Moon had come out of the Sun and Moon islands, just as their human descendants had: The first Inka Manko Qapaq and his wife Mama Oqllo. Therefore, the Sacred Lake was considered as the point of origin of the cosmos and life, in general.

On the different islands, remains of offerings and sacrifices were found, that dated back to pre-Inkan and Inkan periods.

THE UROS' FLOATING ISLANDS

It is an archipelago formed by more than 60 artificial islands made of totora, which are inhabited by the descendants of the Aymara, and not of the Uru ethnic group. That population is mainly devoted to fishing, the elaboration of embroidered carpets and handicraft made of totora, for tourism.

These islands are located within the National Titicaca Lake Reserve, where totora (*seyrpus totora*) is found in abundance.

Floating island model

How do they build a floating island?

- Generally, it is built during the rainy season, because the extraction of the totora root is easier when the water level rises.
- The island's base is a platform rigged with pieces of totora root or kille which are perfectly tied with a resistant rope (Nowadays, nylon is used).
- On the platform, several alternate layers of totora are laid, which, according to the season, climatic factors and use, are being superposed, between 2 and 4 times a month.
- In order to avoid the island's displacement, it is anchored or attached to the lake's bottom, with ropes and eucalyptus poles.

Totora houses

This is a very particular way of life, as it calls the attention of thousands of visitors.

Totora utilization

Totora is used as food, fodder, fuel, fertilizer and building material for the islands, houses, canoes, the elaboration of handicraft, etc.

Titicaca National Reserve

Potato harvest on an island

Totora canoe

Cusco 1920 / (CBC)

CUSCO (3,360 m.a.s.l.)

Cusco's Main Square in Inkan times ▼

Climate			From Lima	Population	
It is very varied and proper to the mountains	Temp.	Max. 22°C	By plane: 1 h. 10 min.	2011: 420,030	Inhab.
		Min. 0°C	By car: 21 h.	2015: 450,095	

There are two seasons in the year:
The rain season offers more steady and warm temperatures, and rainfalls can be frequent and generous, although they are not continuous.
The dry season is characterized by a clear sky, ardent sun and variable temperature which abruptly drops in the shade, and especially during the night.

Cusco is Peru's Historical Capital City, as well as America's Archaeological Capital City, and was declared as Humanity's Cultural Patrimony by the UNESCO, in 1983. It is situated in an ample inter-Andean valley across which small rivers converge to form the Watanay River that, in turn, throws itself into the Urubamba River which has the Amazon River as its final destination.

At the beginning of its history, today's city of Cusco bore the name of Aghamama or Mother Chicha. Later on, the Inkas changed its name and called it Qosqo which means Navel or Center of the World. Qosqo was the capital city of the Tawantinsuyo (Inkan State) and at the same time, it was the Andean world's most important sacred city.

Cusco was restructured by the Inka Pachakuteq who gave it the shape of a puma (Mountain lion or cougar) and divided it in two parts: The Upper Cusco or Hanan Qosqo and the Lower Cusco or Urin Qosqo. The city's center was today's Main Square (Plaza de Armas).

After Francisco Pizarro's arrival, on November 18, 1533, a series of changes took place and in spite of it all, today, Cusco is considered as America's oldest living city, where pre-Hispanic and colonial aspects blend everywhere, with the modern style, and make of it an extraordinary destination.

The Main Square

It was a square divided in two parts: Waqaypata or Hauqaypata and Kusipata.

It was the Center of the Andean World, from which parted the paths (Qhapaq Ñan, Hatun Ñan o Inka Ñan) towards the Four Regions of the Tawantinsuyo.

An intense religious and social activity took place, as the Sun's Feast or Inti Raymi, as well as the reciprocity rite, etc., were celebrated there.

It was covered by sand brought from the Pacific Ocean and surrounded by palaces which displayed the finest architecture. A great part of these buildings was destroyed when the Spanish conquerors distributed the land lots and built new buildings which are a sample of the syncretism or union of two cultures: The Andean and Occidental.

The Cathedral

It took 94 years to build it, because of repeated interruptions. The construction work started on March 11, 1560 and was concluded in July 1654, with stones brought from the Inkan temple of Sacsaywamán and from the Kiswarkancha, the Inkan palace on top of which it was being built.

It is dedicated to Our Lady of the Annunciation.

It shelters many canvas oil paintings, as well as art works in gold and silver, sculptures, etc.

The image of the Black Christ stands out, as he is Cusco's sworn Patron, known as the Lord of Earthquakes.

The Company of Jesus Church

The church that we see today was built in 17 years, between 1651 and 1668.

It is one of the most beautiful ones in Peru and South America. It was built upon the Amarukancha; palace which pertained to the Inka Wayna Qapaq.

It shelters colonial art works, such as paintings from the Cusquenian School of Art, beautiful altars covered with gold sheets, etc.

The wealth in goldsmith works was bounteous, but once the Jesuits were expulsed by the King of Spain, the Crown ordered that all jewels should be requisitioned and sent with their inventory to Spain.

The eradication of idolatries which consisted in the destruction of all forms of Andean belief or religion, to ease the evangelizing work, must have inspired the Vice-kings and Bishops the sculptures, paintings and construction of beautiful churches in order to overshadow the astonishing and superb architectural samples erected by the Inkas.

The Ttwelve Angle Stone

The Twelve Angle Stone is located in Hatunrumiyoq Street's polygonal stone wall and it is part of the palace that belonged to Inka Roka.

In colonial times, it was the house of the first Bishop of Cusco and Peru; Fray Vicente Valverde. Later on, it was the palace of marquis, the Archbishop's Palace, etc. Nowadays, it is the Religious Art Museum.

It is astounding to see the dexterity with which they cut perfect angles, without any other instruments than stone.

107

The Qorikancha or Temple of the Sun

Qorikancha means Golden Enclosure.

Its original name was Intikancha or the "Sun's Enclosure".

It was the Tawantinsuyo's most important and rich Temple of the Sun.

The rooms were dedicated to many divinities, such as The Sun God, Moon, Stars, Lightning, Mother Earth, Water, Rainbow, the God Wiraqocha, the Inkan Emperors' mummies and those of their wives, etc.

Likewise, there was a garden dedicated to the Sun, in which there were plants and animals in full size, made of gold and silver.

When the Spanish came, they distributed the Inkan temples and palaces among themselves and the one who made himself the owner of the Qorikancha, was Juan Pizarro and later on, he donated it to the Dominican Order. Thus, the Dominicans built the Church and Convent of Santo Domingo, which became the oldest in South America.

The Temple of the Sun is one of the most beautiful samples of Inkan architecture.

14 angles in only one perfectly cut stone block, following the inclination of each one of the wall's six planes.

THE SEQ'ES

It is a series of imaginary ritual lines, with astronomical connotations, that divided the territory's physical space, as well as the Inkan society. They parted from the Temple of the Sun and went towards all directions of the Tawantinsuyo, forming the shape of a gigantic sun and on these seq'es, were located the altars and Sacred Places or Wakas attended by the different royal families or panakas.

SAQSAYWAMAN - ROYAL HOUSE OF THE SUN

It is located at 3,555 m.a.s.l.

Sacsaywaman means Satisfied Falcon, although it seems that the more correct interpretation comes from Saqsa = sprinkled or striped and uma = head, which, translated to English, would mean striped head, as it coincides with the puma's head, due to the shape given to the city of Cusco.

It was a great astronomical and religious complex of Hanan Qosqo, which the Inkas called Royal House of the Sun. Thus, it was the Qorikancha's yanantin or complement.

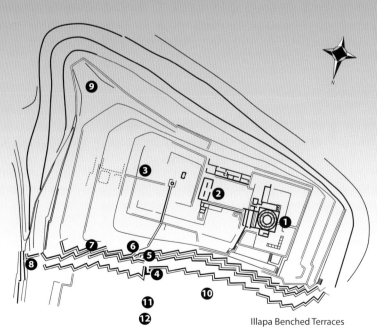

1. Muyuqmarka or Temple of the Sun
2. Sayaqmarka
3. Paukarmarka
4. T'iopunku
5. Akawanapunku
6. Wiraqochapunku
7. Intipunku
8. Pumapunku
9. Vantage Point
10. Chukipampa or Esplanade
11. Suchuna or Slide
12. Qocha or Temple of the Water

Illapa Benched Terraces

The largest stone block weighs more than a 100 tons

Curious design similar to a lama

Representation of the stepped cross symbol, as a magical and religious element

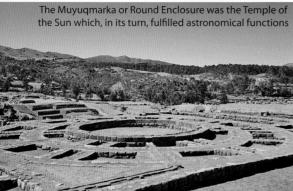

The Muyuqmarka or Round Enclosure was the Temple of the Sun which, in its turn, fulfilled astronomical functions

Saqsaywaman

It was commonly called "fortress", because the conquerors found it similar to European fortresses and above all, because it was the scene of armed conflicts, like for example, the upheaval of Manko Inka II, in 1536, in order to regain control of the Inkan State.

That megalithic architecture was planned and its construction started by the Inka Pachakuteq and concluded by his grandson Wayna Qapaq, and it required the participation of twenty thousand men, during about 70 years.

For its construction, limestone, a sedimentary rock of marine origin, was used, as it was extracted from the place and from nearby quarries.

The three terraces in zigzags would be the physical representation of the ideological concept of lightning in its 3 manifestations: Lightning, its light and thunderbolt. Likewise was the representation of the Pachamama, associated with the concept of division of the universe, in three levels: Hanaq Pacha or the Upper World, the World of Here and the Present or Kay Pacha and the Inner and/or Subterranean World or Ukhu Pacha, identified with the three sacred animals: Condor, Puma and Snake.

This rock outcrop called Suchuna was a Waka or Sacred Place. It might have been ➤ the representation of the Rainbow.

Q'enqo

It is a Quechua word which means Zigzag or Maze.

The Inkas took advantage of a natural calcareous outcrop, for the construction of a great ceremonial center which probably was dedicated to Mother Earth or Pachamama. Thus, it was linked with agrarian and astronomical ritual functions.

This rock has a special aspect, with carstic features, due to the weather and carbonic anhydrite carried by the rain.

Carved altar with ritual functions.

Puka Pukara

Recent denomination which means Red Fort.

It was a center with religious, social and financial functions.

Given its location, it was a traffic control checkpoint. Likewise, it might have been taken advantage of as a warehouse, for agricultural products.

It also has a Sacred Place for ceremonial activities.

Like many other Inkan constructions, it is aesthetically integrated in the landscape, taking advantage of the natural rock formations.

Tambomachay

This Quechua name means Resting Place, although the word mach'ay also means cave which would be related with the ones that can be found there. The caves or caverns were considered as Paqarinas or Places of Origin; in short, Wakas or Sacred Shrines.

Given the features of the place, as far as the surroundings are concerned, as well as the architecture and presence of canals that bring clean and crystalline water from underground sources, Tambomachay had religious functions dedicated to the cult to water. Likewise, it was a water gathering and distribution center, for the area's agricultural irrigation.

The Archaeological Park of Saqsaywaman with 3,093.80 hectares is home for more than 30 archaeological zones.

Sample of the Andean people's knowledge in questions of hydrogeology.

Cusco's Southern Valley

Tipón 1

It is an archaeological complex from the Inkan period, which might have been dedicated to the cult to water, besides having been an agricultural laboratory, where an extraordinary hydraulic engineering system stood out.

The archaeological complexes of Machupicchu and Tipón have been the object of a special recognition, as excellences and jewels of Inkan civil engineering, by the North American Civil Engineers Society (ASCE).

Pikillaqta 2

It is a pre-Inkan walled city built during the Wari culture's apogee (900 a.D.).

In this archaeological park, the city stands out, as it displays a high level of urban planning, with a distribution of spaces, in a geometrical and harmonious design. It presents squares, access ways, sets of enclosures, 1, 2 or 3 floor living quarters, storage rooms, water distribution canals, etc.

Rumiqolqa

It is a stone gateway that was used as a control checkpoint for whoever came from the South and was going in the direction of the city of Cusco. The aqueduct of Lucre's lagoon passed above that gateway, to get to Pikillaqta.

Andahuaylillas

It is a picturesque village in which the church stands out, as it is known as the Andes' Sistine Chapel which was built at the beginning of the 17th century.

Raqchi 3

It is an Inkan archaeological complex located at the foot of the extinct Quinsachata volcano. It was an administrative center in which the temple dedicated to the God Wiraqocha, built in stone and sun-dried mud bricks, stands out. Thus, this complex presents squares, living quarters, qolqas or circular-shaped storage rooms, an artificial water deposit, paths and a fortified wall which surrounds the site.

The Sacred Valley of the Inkas

The geographical space that extends between the localities of San Salvador, Pisaq, Urubamba and Ollantaytambo, along which runs the Urubamba River, is known as the Sacred Valley of the Inkas.

Before the conquerors' arrival, it was the Inkas' favorite place, due to its mild climate, as well as for its natural qualities of beauty and fertility. Its land was intelligently taken advantage of, as it was complemented with an irrigation system and another one of benched terraces that allowed the almost exclusive growing of the best corn called Paraqay sara or giant white corn.

Pisaq

It is a denomination which possibly comes from the Quechua word pisaqa or partridge, gallinacean bird which is abundant in the area. Surprisingly, this archaeological complex has the shape of that bird.

It is a large Inkan administrative center, in which religious, urban, social and financial areas can be distinguished. In addition, it was a traffic checkpoint between the Urubamba Valley and the yunga area or jungle.

This Inkan architectural work achieves the usual harmony with its surroundings and due to its location, it responds to the Andean ideology of proximity to the cosmos.

Colonial Pisaq

This colonial village was built on a broad Inkan terrace, during the 16th century, as the fulfilling of the Ordinance called Indian Reductions (1572) which forced the indigenous people to gather in villages, for a better control, especially of the labor force.

The handicraft market

Originally, it only was a typical market dedicated to the sale of a variety of products. Today, the sale of handicraft products has been incorporated to it, thanks to the visits of tourists. ▶

113

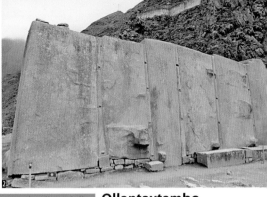

Pinkuylluna hill

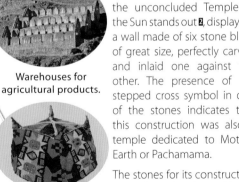

Warehouses for
agricultural products.

Chuku or hat.

Rocks carved in the
shape of human faces

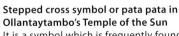

Ollantaytambo

It was a human settlement area, with successive occupation periods. In Inkan times, it was another one of the so many multi-functional "villages"; that is to say that it was an administrative, military, social, economic and religious center. In addition, it is an access checkpoint to several ecological levels.

On the upper part of the so-called fortress ❶, and the most important complex composed of different buildings, in which the unconcluded Temple of the Sun stands out ❷, displaying a wall made of six stone blocs of great size, perfectly carved and inlaid one against the other. The presence of the stepped cross symbol in one of the stones indicates that this construction was also a temple dedicated to Mother Earth or Pachamama.

The stones for its construction were brought from Mount Cachiqhata which is on the other side of the valley.

Stepped cross symbol or pata pata in Ollantaytambo's Temple of the Sun
◀ It is a symbol which is frequently found in the Andean culture and which represents the Earth and cosmos. It can present 3, 5 or 7 ascending and descending levels. It also can be represented by zigzags or terraces.

114

(CS)

Moray

It is a circular system of benched terraces built to take advantage of geological depressions.

They are agricultural terraces that present created microclimates and productive micro-surfaces, with experimental purposes, such as: The domestication, acclimatization or adaptation, watering, etc. of plants.

Salt Mines of Maras

The "Salineras" (Salt Mines) of Maras are exploited since pre-Inkan times and form a compound of about three thousand pools that fill up with salt water that springs forth from natural sources which have their origin in the mountain called Qoripukyu or Golden Springs, as the salt remains ready to be treated and consumed.

Given its location in the Inkas' favorite valley, this salt was exclusively consumed by the Cusquenian elite.

Chinchero

It is a living Inkan village which still conserves its original layout and is located in a very important agricultural area.

The church and tower were built above the Inkan temple's fondations in colonial time.

Likewise, there is a handicraft market, in which textiles, locally manufactured with the use of ancestral techniques, stand out.

Machuqolqa - Inkan warehouses

115

MACHUPICCHU

> "*Machu Picchu revealed itself in front of me, like the reason's existence, above delirium and its inhabitants' absence and that of its creators.*
> *The mystery of its origin and silent tenaciousness, unwound for me the lesson of order the human being can establish through the centuries, with his or her joint will power…*"
>
> ### Pablo Neruda

Machupicchu is one of the few Inkan masterworks which did not suffer excessive alterations, in spite of the passing of time and natural phenomena.

Without a single doubt, it is the most attractive Inkan production, as the best adjectives were used to qualify its beauty and monumental aspect. However, all of them seem to be insufficient, which makes us say: "You have to see it".

The Historical Sanctuary of Machupicchu has been declared as Humanity's Cultural and Natural Patrimony, by the UNESCO, in 1983, and was elected as one of the Seven Wonders of the Modern World, in 2007.

Altitude

The average altitude of the Inkan City of Machupicchu, is 2,450 m.a.s.l.

Climate

It is humid and warm; that is to say, proper to the jungle's edge area.

Annual rainfall varies between 1,571 mm. and 2,381 mm.

- From November to March: 347.9 mm. of monthly rainfall and 90.4% humidity.
- From April to October: 33.8 mm. and 77.2% of relative humidity.

What does the word Machupicchu mean?

Machupicchu is a complex Quechua word which means Old, Ancient or Elder Mountain, and thus is called the mountain on which stands the archaeological complex of the same name.

Vilcabamba Mountain Range

Where is Machupicchu located?

The Inkan City of Machupicchu is situated North-west of the city of Cusco, in the District of Machupicchu, Province of Urubamba and Department of Cusco.

It lies between 13°9'47" of latitude South and 72°32'34" of longitude West, with a magnetic decline of 2°54' West.

Geographically speaking, it is located between the Andes and the Amazon Basin, on granite rocks of Vilcabamba's Batholith, on the mountainous massif of Machupicchu.

The Historical Sanctuary of Machupicchu is a perfect environment, in which unique ecosystems have developed. It encompasses 13 life zones and an extraordinary biological diversity.

Boissonneaua matthewsii
Brown-breasted hummingbird

Some antecedents to the scientific discovery:

- Undoubtedly, it had great importance at the time of the Inkan apogee. Stage in which this Inkan city was built.
- Possibly, the area of Machupicchu was known in a limited way, during the colonial period, and it would have been the object of pillage on the part of extirpators of idolatry and others.
- The area where the Inkan City of Machupicchu is located, is mentioned with different denominations and was the property of different people, since the Colony, and all the way to the Agrarian Reform.

Gloxinia sylvatica

Bromeliaceae

Small lizard

Vizcacha

- In 1867, Machupicchu would have been discovered by the German adventurer Augusto Berns who had no scientific or archaeological interest at all.
- There is a map of the Sanctuary's exact location, in the archives of Lima's National Library, drawn by German Göhring, in December of 1874.
- On July 14, 1902, the Inkan City of Machupicchu was visited by Enrique Palma, Gabino Sánchez and Agustín Lizárraga.
- It is obvious that Machupicchu was known way before that, but, unfortunately, no one gave it any importance, and less still, did they make it be known.

The North American professor Hiram Bingham, undertook the adventure, with the intention of seeking the Inkas' last capital city, the lost city of Manko Qapaq II and his successors or the chroniclers' Vilcabamba, at the time of Toledo (Vice King of Peru, between 1569 and 1581).

H. Bingham revised different researchers' documents and maps, like those of Charles Wiener, Antonio Raymondi and Sir Clement Markham, among others.

Thanks to a previous research (He had certain knowledge of the existence of Machupicchu), and to the help he received from authorities and individuals, he managed to get to the monument.

Who made the scientific discovery of Machupicchu and when?

Who officially discovered that city, was the Latin American History Professor from Yale University, in Massachusetts, USA, and North American explorer, Hiram Bingham, on July 24, 1911. That day, he went up accompanied by Melchor Arteaga and Sergeant Carrasco, and was welcomed by Anacleto Álvarez and Toribio Recharte who were living in the architectural complex of Machupicchu, and grew their corn on the Inkan benched terraces.

The young boy Melquiades Recharte, better known as Pablito, guided Professor Hiram Bingham to that important architectural testimony in humanity's history, which was rapidly made known to the whole world.

He made the existence of Machupicchu public, through thousands of pictures.

Hiram Bingham (CE)

Temple of the Sun (HB)

It was protected by Mother Nature, during almost 400 years.

Precarious bridge over the Urubamba River, to ascend to Machupicchu

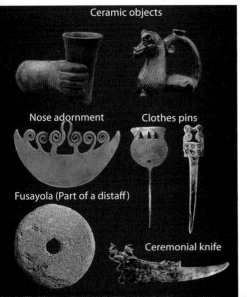

Ceramic objects

Nose adornment

Clothes pins

Fusayola (Part of a distaff)

Ceremonial knife

What was found in the excavations undertaken by Hiram Bingham?

The 1912 expedition was organized by Yale University and the National Geographic Society, with the aim of complementing and continuing studies on the topography, geology, meteorology and bones, along with anthropological and archaeological studies undertaken by the 1911 expedition.

After cleansing the dense vegetation, they obtained maps, went around the place, undertook excavations and found a great quantity of objects:

- Copper and bronze objects (Chisels, pickaxes and levers), as well as silver objects.
- Pieces of ceremonial and domestic ceramics.
- Objects made of stone: Hundreds of rounded edge stones, percussion stones, hematite and others still.
- Remains of wood.
- Some objects in the making.
- Micro sculptures.
- Green crystal beads, peach pips and a cattle bone (European origin).

From that discovery, very few are the pieces exposed in Machupicchu's Museum, at the Casa Concha, in Cusco.

Many other pieces salvaged thanks to the last research are on display at the Manuel Chávez Ballón Site Museum located at the foot of the Inkan City of Machupicchu.

In addition, the following were found:

107 tombs were found, in which there were bone remains of 173 individuals, of which, few seem to have pertained to the elite. In these tombs were found a series of offerings (Earthen vessels, adornments in silver, copper, bone or stone, as well as remains of lamas, dogs and guinea pigs).

According to the initial bone remain analysis made by Bingham and G. Eaton, there were more individuals of the feminine gender. But, according to the last bone studies made by Jhon Verano, in 2003, one gets to the conclusion that there was certain homogeneity between both sexes.

In the upper cemetery, seven of the most important tombs were found.

90% of the tombs were found in the peripheral part of the city; that is, only 10%, inside it.

What was Machupicchu and what function did it have?

There are many hypothesis and interpretations at hand.

However, one can infer that it was an important "llaqta" or multi-functional Inkan city.

It mainly was a magical and religious nucleus, as well as a great solar worshipping sanctuary, as its extraordinary surroundings and the quantity of buildings erected there, favor this purpuse.

Furthermore:

- It was a dynamic administrative center, with public spaces, places for religious worshipping, handicraft specialization points, as well as residential and agricultural areas.
- Because of its strategic location, it was the capital city of Cusco's inter-tropical area, important for its natural resources (Coca leaf, hot pepper, medicinal plants, feathers, gold, silver, etc.).

Sacred Rock or Waka, beneath which one of the most interesting tombs was found, which belonged to a high ranking woman who was buried with pomp and ostentation. In that tomb, personal objects were found, as well as ceramic objects, the skeleton of a dog, etc.

(GE) 1916

In 1995, a star-shaped "porra" (Andean weapon) in its melting process, was found.
In 1996, a 16 karat gold bracelet was found, as the only gold piece discovered on the site.

It is situated in a cloud forest and surrounded by dense vegetation.

- It was a power center, a key site for traffic, access control, mediation and interchange between the high Andean territories and the Amazon.
- It was a mark of possession, and part of a set of protagonist villages, in the broad area that was being conquered by the Inkas who had the intention of expanding their territorial, and especially, agricultural borders. They were avid of knowledge which, to them, was a source of power.
- It was a research and specialization center, in diverse activities.
- It was an astronomical observation center. Thanks to the mountains' proximity and verticality.
- It was a study and biological diversity experimentation center, through the handling of different altitudinal levels and creation of various ecosystems, to grow diverse species of flora (Agricultural laboratory).

Research undertaken by Mereida Puma Soria and Carlos Ayme Carrasco, shows that the so-called existence of "private estates", was all part of the manipulation strategies used by the Spanish, to adjudicate these properties to their king, and favor the Spanish Crown. Therefore, the hypothesis which sustains that Machupicchu was a private property, farm or resting home of the Inka Pachakuteq, is to be abandoned as being incorrect.

The Inkan edifications fulfill a variety of functions related to religious activities, as well as to administrative ones, control and so on.

The effective use of spaces leads to the inexistence of structures strictly reserved to control or to any other specific function.

As an established pattern, every place had to have an area destined to ceremonial activities.

Machupicchu is a city which is in accordance with its time, as well as with the needs and situation of the moment.

The Inkan City of Machupicchu is part of the 196 archaeological sites in the Historical Sanctuary which covers 32,592 hectares.

When was Machupicchu built?

Its construction pertains to the Inkan apogee's time period, during the second half of the 15th century. The city was designed by the Inka Pachakuteq and its construction started during his government.

It took place at a stage in that period, in which building was a specialized activity that involved highly developed processes and technologies, and furthermore, it was a historical moment in which there were great surplus of all kinds of resources.

This monumental work probably was initiated between 1450 and 1460 a.D

The Inka Pachakuteq imagined it, but never saw it as we know it today, as its construction lasted for several generations.

It presents a rough terrain, with very steep slopes.

Where is it built?

The Inkan City of Machupicchu is built in a very special place, on a very different ecological level than others on which the Inkas used to build, and above all, in a very rough place, and even so, they chose an area of lesser vulnerability.

The place where the city is built, is the result of the collapsing of two huge geological faults: That of Machupicchu and the other, of Huaynapicchu.

The city of Machupicchu is strategically located in a region that was quite populated. Therefore, it was surrounded by nearby satelite supplying places, with their own characteristics and categories, and is linked through a well developed trail network.

It is the result of an unbelievable project and a challenge with impressive characteristics.

In Inkan times, the Urubamba River or Willkamayu, was venerated in the same way as the Celestial River or Milky Way.

The Sacred River surrounds and protects it, in complicity with the precipices and strong wall that runs all the way to the Inti Punku.

How was it built?

The planning study probably lasted for years, in order to achieve a project that would ensure the comfortable, healthy and safe development of activities of the people who were going to inhabit it.

The Inkan engineers and architects who imagined, designed, planned and built it, conceived it as a functional whole, fulfilling the exigencies of balance, stability, resistance and aesthetics.

They had a full and minutious knowledge of the geography and topography of the area in which they decided to establish that strategic location.

They knew and understood the conditions of the soil, the environmental factors with which the construction would interact, and how it would respond to the above mentioned factors.

They especially studied the annual movement of the Sun (Sunrise, trajectory, sunset, days of zenithal sun, etc.) and, finally, the celestial sphere.

They identified the most important resources for its construction: Water and stone material.

Just one water supply canal for the city.

◀ Stone in its setting process. In order for it to fit onto the lower stone, they should have removed the wedge.

Execution of the construction work

- They cleared the vegetation that covered the granite chaos and identified the surface stones **1** that could be used as building materials, as well as the bedrocks, as a base for building.
- They made the water canal **2**.
- They built sustainment terraces, giving special attention to the drainage system. These terraces were built on the mountain slope, from the bottom up.
- On top of these sustainment terraces, they built the different enclosures which, in their majority, were made with smaller stones **3**.

This wall clearly displays two types of building materials and techniques, and the presence of the drainage canal, serves as a boundary between both the terrace and enclosure. ▼

Building of sustaining terraces

The foundations are perfectly "rooted" on a uniformly resistant soil, for which they mainly used the base rock (Bedrock).

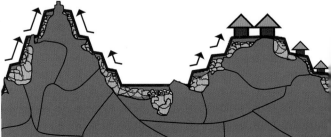

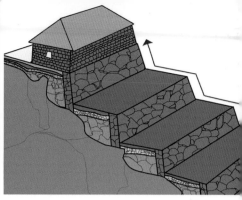

The walls' first layer is seated and set upon concave spaces. The convexe shape of each superposed stone, allows a perfect fit, giving balance, solidity and stability to the structure, which are qualities that are consolidated by the inclination of the walls.

The contention and sustainment walls are built with large wedged stones, and then, the spaces that are left between these and the mountain, are filled with stones that are found nearby and on higher areas, as well as with residual material, until the terraces are complete.

The architectural structure of the city of Machupicchu, is perfectly built, so as to face the constant challenge of gravity and to withstand loads due to water pressure, as well as those of the soil and earthquake pressure.

It is considered that the underground work performed (Foundations, drainage canals, landfills, etc.) amounts to more than 50% of the construction's total work.

The use of natural, smoothened, cut or carved stones, corresponded to the function given to the construction.

What building materials were used?

Mainly, the granite chaos or stone fields were used which were on the site. These rocks break apart from their nucleus, due to the action of natural phenomena, through time.

Granite has conditions to be a good building material, given its iron sulphur-free composition and the presence of intertwined disjunctions which allow the splitting of the rocks into polygonal blocks.

Likewise, clay, gravel, sand and fertile soil were carried from the bottom of gorges and valleys.

The magnetic intrusion process and contractions suffered by rocks, in their cooling stage, originated natural fractures.

They had to bring soil, sand and clay, in order to fill benched terraces, squares, paths, etc.

Example of a construction leaning against the sustainment terrace. The lack of fixtures can clearly be observed. ▶

Where does the water that supplies Machupicchu spring from?

The main water spring **1** that permanently provides water to that city, is located South of the archaeological complex, at an altitude of 2,458.5 m.a.s.l. and it descends to 2,436.4 m.a.s.l.

Rain water infiltration through geological faults was recollected, to supply the city, by means of a main canal **2** that extends over 760 m., with a nominal capacity of 300 liters per minute.

The presence of geological faults guarantees the abundance of aquifer deposits, and vegetation reduces runoff waters and increases their infiltration.

Hydrogeologists sustain that the spring is a great underground water reservoir which is supplied each year, during the rain season, and therefore, there always is water.

Regarding hydraulic engineering, the calculation and projection towards the future, are extraordinary.

Building a city like Machupicchu, based on a simple water spring, would have been too risky.

The water spring **1** determined the distribution and spatial order of Machupicchu's architectural complex.

How many inhabitants were there in Machupicchu?

Given the number of enclosures used as living quarters, deduction can be made that it was inhabited by families, with a total of about 500 individuals pertaining, in their majority, to the Inkan elite, and there is evidence that people of other ethnic groups (Qolla, Chimú and Lupaca) also lived there, and were dedicated to worship and research.

When was Machupicchu abandoned?

Possibly, will it ever be known neither when, nor in which circumstances that city was abandoned.

However, parting from the hypothesis that the existence of Machupicchu was known by a small and exclusive group of people belonging to the highest Inkan hierarchic level, and given its extraordinary importance, it was decided to maintain its existence as a secret during the conquest.

The main canal that goes to the first fountain, possibly was the first construccion work they undertook, in a temporary way, as they built it with small stones. But, in order to avoid loss of water, they had planned to repair and resolve this problem, substituting the small stones by other stones of a larger size and excellent cut; reason for which there are 38 large cut stones.

When Manko Inka rose in arms, to reconquer the Tawantinsuyo, in 1536, order might have been given to abandon Machupicchu. The escape must have been massive and hastened, with the immediate incursion of its inhabitants in the Amazonian jungle.

Furthermore, decision was made to destroy bridges, and especially, the path which was reopened later on, to ease the official discovery of Machupicchu.

On the other hand, it is probable that, with the early and fast spread of smallpocks which originated civil war, the Inkan city might have remained very much weakened, in the same way as was the whole of the Tawantinsuyo, and that great desorganization might have left it almost without resources, in all senses of the word, and later on, the conquest would have forced its last inhabitants to leave it.

There are people who believe that the Inkas left the city after 1540, because the Spanish decidedly penetrated in those steep mountain territories, during their military campaign against the Inkas.

What is the main secret to which its long existence is due?

The greatest deterioration can be caused by rainfall, and so, the secret or most important element is the drainage system which, along with the foundations, constituted more than 50% of the effort made in the construction of Machupicchu, to ensure its durability.

Likewise, the benched terraces that surround it help its long and secure existence.

The Inkas used faults and cracks that naturally favor drainage, for the construction of water elimination and circulation canals.

The drainage system is composed of the dry moat **1**, as well as of different kinds of canals that can be longitudinal, caves **2** used for drainage, slanted horizontal surfaces or drainage canals combined with stairways, sidewalks, etc.

All exposed surfaces are slightly slanted towards the outside, and thus, water will never form pools there, no matter how torrential the rainfall might be.

There is an extraordinary drainage system, to avoid infiltrations that could cause disastrous sinking due to the structures' weight.

There are over one hundred drainage canals that run across the city.

127

How is space distributed in Machupicchu?

In the same way as other Inkan cities or llaqtas, this one also follows the principles of duality and quatri-partition.

It is divided into two main sectors: The urban and agricultural which are separated by the dry moat. Each one of these sectors is then divided into two sub-sectors: The Upper or Hanan and Lower or Urin, which represent 19 urban compounds (Residential quarters of the nobility and specialists, temples, wakas, workshops, storage rooms and others), 13 agricultural compounds, a central square, 2 smaller squares and 8 trails.

The Eastern side of Machupicchu, presents little over 60% of the whole of its constructions.

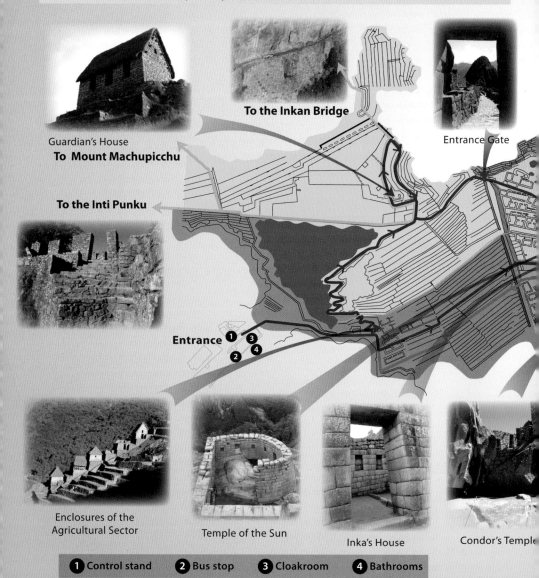

To the Inkan Bridge

Entrance Gate

Guardian's House
To Mount Machupicchu

To the Inti Punku

Entrance ❶ ❸
❷ ❹

Enclosures of the Agricultural Sector

Temple of the Sun

Inka's House

Condor's Temple

❶ Control stand   ❷ Bus stop   ❸ Cloakroom   ❹ Bathrooms

There are 183 enclosures of which 108 have a rectangular layout with 1 (39 %), 2, 3, 4, 10 and 12 access ways; 03 of a floor and a half; 12 of two floors; 31 wayranas; 03 of semicircular layout; 10 of circular layout and the others are wakas, underground spaces and different enclosures.

Machupicchu was erected in relation to the Sun and its trajectory through the firmament. Each space built is oriented in order to receive the greatest amount of solar light and heat, during more hours per day, and every day of the year.

The city's distribution goes from East to West and from North to South, as it connects with a sacred landscape, in which snow-capped mountains can be seen in the distance, as well as other nearby ones that coincide with the four cardinal directions.

Sacred Square

Intiwatana

To Huaynapicchu

Sacred Rock

Three Doorways' Compound

Astronomical Mirrors

| ROUTES |
| GOING |
| RETURNING |
| ALTERNATIVE CIRCUIT |

Upper Agricultural Sector   **Lower Agricultural Sector**

Upper Urban Sector   **Lower Urban Sector**

The Urban Sector

After a comparative study, deduction was made that the Inkan City of Machupicchu follows the same urban planning criteria as that of the city of Cusco in Inkan times, with subtle modifications and adaptations to the topography.

Upper Urban Sector
Compound 1

It is composed of the entrance, deposits **1**, living quarters, patios or vantage points, a watch post and a "waka" or ceremonial building **2**.

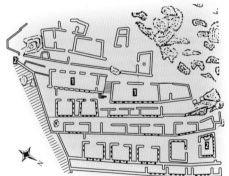

- **The Entrance Gate**

  It was an access way to the Urban Sector, by the main trail.

  That portal **3** was restored and it is equipped with a system to restrict access **4**.

Compound 2

This compound was the city's most important ceremonial place, because it synthesized the Andean cosmogonic vision.

It is composed of the Temple of the Sun, Mother Earth's Temple or Royal Tomb, the "Wayrana" or three-walled ceremonial enclosure, four fountains and other enclosures.

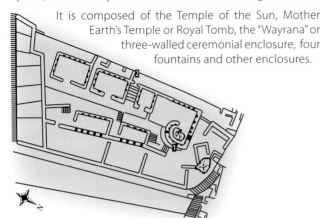

winter solstice

• The Temple of the Sun

It is a fine architecture or imperial style semicircular structure built on top of bedrock which serves as its base and altar.

Given the characteristics it displays, it also was an astronomical observatory, with calendar setting purposes.

The window directed towards the North-east, allows the observation of the winter solstice. That is to say that, each June 21, the first ray of the Sun directly enters through that window **1** and projects its light upon the carved rock which was related with two other windows that allow stellar observation.

During the days of the winter solstice, in the early morning, one can appreciate the constellation of the Pleiades (Qolqa), through this window.

The Temple of the Sun was also used to predict the passing of the Sun through the zenith.

The only access to the Temple of the Sun presents a double jamb door **2** and restricted access features **3**, proper to very important places.

The protuberance which is in the extreme right, projects a shadow which fits in that cavity, at 10:00 a.m., on the day of the winter solstice.

The shadows of each one of the upper protuberances get superposed to those projected by the lower ones, thus forming two parallel lines; a phenomenon that can be observed, after 12 noon, during the passing of the Sun through the zenith. It is believed that they might have been used to hold some object that helped in astronomical observations.

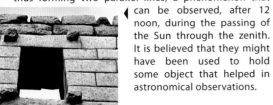

A fine wall underground cubicle was found in the Temple of the Sun. Given its characteristics, it can be assumed that it was associated with ceremonial functions. Although the absence of cultural material during the excavation leads one to believe that it was never used and that it possibly belonged to the group of abandoned and buried constructions.

During the excavations performed in the circled rooms, great quantities of broken ceramics and carved stones were found along with ashes. It is believed that this discovery is related to the abandoning process of the city, since its inhabitants were unable to take their belongings along and decided to break and burn them.

- ## Mother Earth's Temple or Royal Tomb ❶

  Given its location (Under the Temple of the Sun), and the presence of the stepped cross symbol ❷, it was a temple dedicated to Mother Earth or Pachamama and a "Paqarina" or Place of Origin.

  It probably was destined to shelter the remains of a very important individual or a representation of him, in spite of showing evidence that it hadn't been used. Upon Bingham's arrival, it had already been profaned.

  Nevertheless, the stone sculpture ❸ that is inside this enclosure shows stains of still unknown substances, which demonstrates that it was a ceremonial place.

  This temple, unique for the quality of its architectural finish, shows perfect harmony, balance and complementarity ❹ between nature and the human being's work.

132

132

- **The Fountains**

  There are 16 interconnected fountains that carry the water, to supply the population.

  The third fountain  has the best finish and it was dedicated to the cult to water, an element conceived as a substantial resource, which flows between the three worlds and gives its origin to life.

  This fountain fulfilled ceremonial functions, along with the window which presents perforations, and the construction with three walls and a roof, called "wayrana".

  These fountains are interconnected by canals designed with extraordinary precision, so that the water might flow with little infiltration and in a controled manner.

Several fountains, as well as canals are sculpted in the bedrock.

Compound 3

This compound is known under the denomination of the Inka's House.

It is a residential compound of the "kancha" type, which includes bedrooms, patios, mortars, "wayranas", a warehouse, a kitchen and a stone sculpture at the entrance.

- **The Inka's House 2**

  Its layout, structure, location and the architecture with fine finish presented by the enclosures in the main patio, and especially, their location nearby the Temple of the Sun and water fountains, allow us to assert that it was a residential compound for high ranking individuals.

  In the vestibule of the Inka's House, there is a bedrock presenting a very well carved orifice 3 probably used for astronomical ends. This orifice projects a circular light on the floor, at noon, on October 30 and February 14 (Average days of the passing of the Sun by the zenith).

  Stairs 4 located South of the Inka's House Compound - 1911. ▶

In the space situated on the Eastern side of the Inka's House, a fine underground wall was found that probably responded to design changes, as a consequence of movement which originated the structural settling that weakened the place.
There are some underground structures like these.

The Quarry **1**

This area is situated between compound 1 and 4. In the same way as in another similar one, although smaller, situated in the compound 6, it is known as quarry. Apart from providing the stone material, these places were in construction when the city was abandoned.

There are some walls in their building process among the granite chaos, while on the Western side, there is a double jamb doorway with finely cut stones, also in its building process. One of the bedrocks **2**, which served as a foundation for the building, shows the slightly concave setting joint carving, to set the next slightly convex stones in place, and guarantee their adjusting and resistance.

The presence of circular constructions **3** stands out in the quarry area. These were built as temporary homes for the city's stone cutters and builders.

Similar constructions were found in the Agricultural Compound's upper part.

There probably were many similar structures in the whole area now occupied by the city, which were destroyed, as the final construction progressed.

Machupicchu's dump is located on the quarries' Southern side, between 40 and 50 m. down below, where nearly 10,000 fragments of ceramics, ashes, carbon, broken grinding stones, etc., were found, which are refuse that show the city's continuity through time.

The Inkan City of Machupicchu was built, modifying very subtly the "Granite Chaos" (Stones of different sizes that break off from the bedrock, in a disorderly way).

The presence of geological faults guarantees abundant construction materials.

Compound 4

It is known as the Temples' Compound, the urban pattern of which is of the "kancha" type. Around the patio, known as "The Sacred Square", are the Main Temple, the Temple of the Three Windows or Mother Earth's Temple, the Priest's House and the base of an incomplete semi-circular temple.

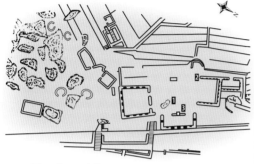

- **The Sacred Square**

  It was a space in which particular ceremonies were performed.

  In one of the excavations, a subterranean burial cave was found. Given the findings, it is asserted that the tomb belonged to a woman of high status.

  In this square, a stone **1** in its carrying and smoothening process, stands out, as well as a stone sculpture representing the Chakana or Southern Cross **2** which is a stone compass as well.

  Likewise, there is the basis of an unconcluded semicircular temple of fine architecture.

- **The Three Windows' Temple**

  It was dedicated to the cult to the Pachamama, given the presence of the stepped cross symbol **3**.

  Its orientation was taken into account and on June 21, the Sun's rays enter through the three windows, producing a projection of symmetrical shadows.

  Outside and beneath the windows, a great quantity of remains of decorated ceramics was found.

This temple was in its finishing process, in the same way as were some others. For example, the outer sides **1** bear marks, to smoothen and polish them. Likewise, there are two closed windows **2** converted into niches, and one of them still seems to have been in its carving process **3**.

- **The Main Temple 4**

This temple displays one of the finest construction styles, called Imperial Inka.

Given its orientation, it probably was a place of stellar observation, since, from that point, one can contemplate great part of the Milky Way, and especially, the Southern Cross.

In the same way, it might have been a temple dedicated to Sacred Mountains (Apus Salkantay and Machupicchu), as these were the deities that provided water.

The dislocation and slight sinking towards the East, in the temple, is the consequence of a rock displacement by gravity, caused by rainwater infiltration.

There are geological faults which have not suffered from recent earth movements. In general terms, there is no danger due to earthquake faults that could put Machupicchu's architectural integrity at risk.

For example, the earthquakes that took place in 1950 and 1986, related with faults that run South of the Sanctuary, did not affect the city of Machupicchu.

At the back of the Main Temple, there is an unfinished enclosure of finely cut stones, from which one can appreciate the Apu Mount Pumasillo **5 6**.

One can see Pachamama's symbol **7** on the entrance way's lateral stones, as the representation of the Three Worlds: Hanaq Pacha, Kay Pacha and Ukhu Pacha.

◀ Main Temple and uncomplete semi-circular temple.

Compound 5

This compound is known as the "Intihuatana" or "Solar Clock". It is a stone sculpture that was located on top of a hill which, in turn, was almost totally covered by sustainment walls .

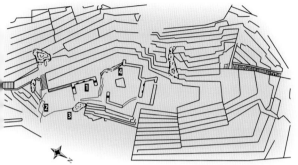

One can only access this compound, using the stairs that run from the Temples' Compound. On the upper part, there is a three-leveled platform.

To the South of the first level, there is a stone ring ❷ which lets the sunlight go through it perpendicularly, when the Sun is in its zenith.

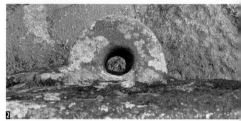

On the second level, to the East of the wayrana, there is a "Waka" or Sacred Rock ❸ which is important for its shape, similar to that of mounts Huaynapicchu and Putukusi, as well as that of the Urubamba River.

On the highest level, there is the Intiwatana.

- **The Intiwatana**

  In Inkan times, this kind of instrument was known as Saywa or Sukanka which means astronomical pillar.

  It is a religious and astronomical element, carved with many facets and angles which, as they are being illuminated, as much by solar, as by lunar light, project shadows that were interpreted for calendar setting purposes.

  On the Western side, there is a stairway built there to allow the observation of the winter solstice.

  On June 21, the Sun rises at 7:20 a.m., and projects a triangular beam of light ❹ inside which a little circle carved in low-relief, stands out.

The upright protuberance does not project any shadow, at the moment in which the Sun is at its zenith, which takes place on October 30 and February 14 (Average days).

Likewise, the horizontal prominence projects a shadow on the lower part, conserving its same length, at the moment the Sun enters its zenith.

In this coumpound's wayranas, there are two closed windows **1 2** as an answer to changes made in the design, during the building process.

During the winter solstice, the Sun rises with an azimuth of 66°, and sets in a manmade depression, on top of Mount San Miguel or Wiskacha, with an azimuth of 300°25'.

During the summer solstice, the Sun rises from a point close to the Inti Punku, with an azimuth of 112°, and sets on the summit of the snow-capped Mount Pumasillo, with an azimuth of 249°.

The Sun has an apparent trajectory between 66° (Winter solstice – June 21) and 112° (Summer solstice – December 22).

Winter Solstice

Anti-Zenith or Nadir

Equinoxes

Zenith

Summer Solstice

Lower Urban Sector
Compound 6

It bears the denomination of "Sacred Rock" or Mother Earth's Temple. It is a "kancha" with a patio around it in which there are two "wayranas" and the Sacred Rock.

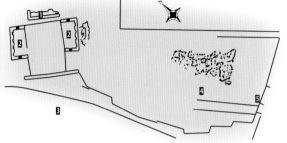

- **The Sacred Rock**

  It is a natural rock that had a ceremonial function, the base of which is made with carved stones, as it is similar to the profile of the mountain called Yanantin.

  There are two enclosures or wayranas ❷ on either side of this Waka, which were built with small stones and mud mortar. These structures were coated and plastered with a light ocher color.

  Clay mixed with fine sand and straw was used to achieve this coating.

  This enclosure's floor is slightly slanted towards the outside, as it ends in a canal, in order to avoid the intrusion or stagnation of rain water.

  To the West, there are the only agricultural terraces ❸ in a sunk space, that must have been one of the agricultural experimentation centers.

  To the South, on the upper part, there are contention walls of fine architecture, on top of which there is the second quarry which rather was a place in the process of being built.

  Here, there is a radial petroglyph ❹ which has incisions displaying 16 lines that irradiate from a central point. It seems to have been a representation of the set of imaginary lines called "seq'e".

  Calling on curiosity, one can see the outline of a bird in flight, on one of the contention walls ❺.

Compound 7, 8 and 9

There are kancha-type buildings, with "wayranas" and living quarters.

The Three Doorways' Compound stands out.

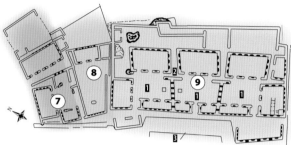

- **The Three Doorways' Compound 1**

  It was a living quarters' compound with an excellent location that allowed it to catch the Sun's rays throughout the day and all year long, but it was far away from the water fountains.

  These constructions of the "kancha" type, present an entrance way that leads to a central patio, around which living quarters and enclosures with three walls are distributed.

  The three "kanchas" or enclosures are interconnected by means of a skillfully traced narrow passage way 2.

  Below the Three Doorways' Compound 3, is the place related with the Square, where excavations took place and a great quantity of large jars, plates and drinking vessels called "keros" of different sizes, were found. It also is probable that it might have been related with ceremonies performed at the moment of abandoning the city or it might perhaps have been the result of some kind of ritual in which the breaking of objects took place.

  The Main Square is situated South-west of this compound.

The Main Square

Like any other Inkan square, it was a place for ceremonial and social activities.
Given its size, it can be deduced that quite a lot of people used to participate in popular events and ceremonies, as it offers an excellent acoustic quality.

Imagining men breaking stones, transporting, cutting, polishing and setting them…, brings us to reflect upon this kind of work which, indeed, required much organization, labor force, dexterity, wisdom and patience, and all of it for a spiritual reward.

Compound 10, 11 and 12

In this compound, the "kallanca" stands out, as a 26 meter long and 10 meter wide construction which is the largest in the city, in addition to the warehouses and a rocky outcrop that stands out, which has a ritual meaning and is called "Waka".

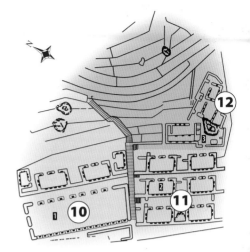

- **The Kallanka 1**

  It is Machupicchu's largest room and was used to accommodate a large number of people. During the day, it might have been used for collective work, and possibly, for other activities, because it is next to an open space.

- **The Qolqas or Storage Rooms 2**

  These are constructions with two symmetrical floors, in their shape and disposition.

  Their location and proximity to the agricultural benched terraces on the lower part, makes us believe that they were warehouses for agricultural products.

The magnitude of the construction work required great quantities of food, clothes, tools, etc., carried along by hundreds of men and women.

- **The Waka (Carved Rock) 3**

  There are many rocks like this one which were used as altars or ceremonial spaces.

  In the upper part, the step-like symbol is carved with flat surfaces, which indicates that it was a ceremonial altar.

  The Waka was used for funeral ritual purposes. Indeed, below it 4, three tombs were found, among which, one stands out, that belonged to an important woman. The most outstanding objects, as part of the tombs, are a variety of stone, bone and ceramic "fusayolas" (Parts of distaffs). Around that "waca", they built small subterranean enclosures.

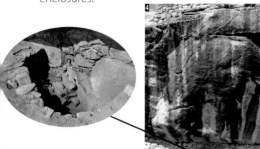

Compound 13

In this compound, there are rectangular enclosures, some of which have two floors, with access to the first floor, by means of inner stairs. Here, the construction called "Intimach'ay" stands out.

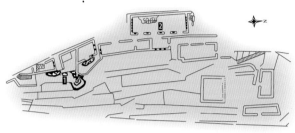

- ### The Intimach'ay ❶

  It is a small cave used for astronomical observation.

  This cavity is completely lit by the Sun, only on the summer solstice, when the sunlight enters by the window, on the left hand side. There is no doubt that the astronomical observation from that point, was made days before and after the event, since the city of Machupicchu is located in a rainy area with quite a lot of clouds.

  This neighborhood's largest building ❷ has two floors and the stairway that interconnects them is built, taking advantage of a rocky outcrop in the place.

Compound 14, 15 and 16

Between the compounds 14 and 15, a rock of ceremonial importance, stands out. It is a "Waka" ❸ which is part of a "Kancha".

Compound 16 is known as the "Mortars' Compound" or "Compound of the Astronomical Mirrors".

All of these compounds formed a ceremonial sector, given the presence of fine buildings equipped with beautifull stairs ❹, double jamb entrances ❺ and restricted access systems. In addition, several of them shelter ceremonial altars.

◄ This is one of Bingham's pictures showing one of the buildings in this sector, with remains of dense vegetation.

• The Astronomical Mirrors' Room or Mortars' Room ■

In the central part and on this enclosure's ground level, there are two bedrock stones carved in a circular shape, both of almost the same diameter. These are two water mirrors, with an astronomical function. The one that points to the North might have been used to observe equinoxes, and the other mirror was there to detect winter solstices.

The inter-diametrical axis marks exactly the North and South poles, thus turning itself into a compass.

There are some enclosures that present remains of red and yellow paint ■ ■.

Compound 17

The Condor's Temple stands out. However, there are wakas and buildings with particular features, such as the polygonal enclosure ■ that has a rock as its base which, in turn, presents a small cave that facilitates rainwater runoff.

In the same compound, there is a large natural rock erroneously known as the slide ■. In reality, this rock also was a ceremonial place; that is to say, a waka.

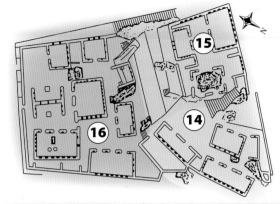

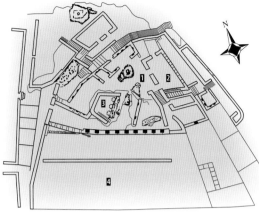

- **The Condor's Temple**

Natural rocks were used with great genius, to make this symbolic representation of the condor flying off, in such a way that it was a sector for religious and astronomical use, related to the sunrise between April 20 and 24, and August 16 and 20 (Anti-zenith or nadir).

The condor's head and neck were sculpted in a superficial rock.

In its lower part, there is a cave where household and ceremonial ceramics were found, along with cameloid and guinea pig bones.

Underneath the wings, there is an excellent structural stabilizing work. Likewise, inside, one can appreciate a niche of fine architecture, which shows the ritual importance of the place.

To the East of the temple, there is a building which has two floors. On the first floor, there are evidences that guinea pigs were raised there. It is only by passing through this room, that one can have access to the sixteenth water fountain which is separated from the others by a wall.

In the upper part of the temple, there is a ceremonial altar, with niches probably related to worshiping the dead.

On the Western side, the third square is located, where there actually is a Pisonay tree. On this square, an excavation was made in 1994, and an underground contention wall was found that served to avoid the displacement of refuse material from the construction process, used as landfill.

One single gold object was found there as well, which might have belonged to one of the architects.

144

Compound 18 and 19

Both compounds are known as the "Popular Group".

There are rooms with one and two floors, which served as living quarters, and others, as deposits.

These compounds occupy the lower zone East of the city of Machupicchu. The topography of the place is quite irregular, but even so, it was very well exploited, and these compounds require a research and restoration project.

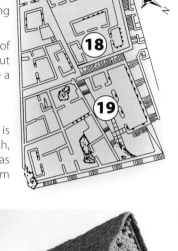

The Agricultural Sector

This sector is mainly situated to the South of the city, and is complemented with several compounds around it, which, undoubtedly, fulfilled an agricultural function and also served as contention walls for the soil, as well as to protect the buildings from falling down. There also are ceremonial and ornamental terraces.

One of the ceremonial terraces is located in the upper part of the Agricultural Sector, in which there is the wayrana known as The Guardian's House and The Sacrifice Rock or Funerary Rock.

• The Guardian's House

It is a well ventilated and illuminated roofed construction with three walls, or wayrana, which is located on the upper part of the Agricultural Sector, allowing a broad and full view of the surrounding area. This room also seems to have had control and astronomical functions. At sunrise, on June 21 of each year, symmetrical shadows are being projected through the three windows.

The few examples of roofs in Machupicchu, are reconstructions, as the original ones were destroyed with the passing of time.

• The Sacrifice Rock

It is called that way, although there is no evidence whatsoever of this. However, it fulfilled a ceremonial function and was also used for astronomical observation.

This slightly slanted orifice on its Eastern side projects an oval light, only at noon, on the day of the winter solstice.

Near that rock, there is an "Apacheta", which is a conglomeration of small stones of up to nine different kinds, that were brought there as offerings.

- **Agricultural Terraces**

As a result of the pollen and spores' analysis performed on several soil samples proceeding from the terraces, it is known that the inhabitants grew corn, coca, virraca, quinoa, potatoes, achira, zucchini, granadilla, beans, avocado, small tomatoes, medicinal plants and others.

The building technology used for agricultural benched terraces (Internal structure, location, drainage system, etc.) has allowed the Inkas to maintain a fertile soil, with all of its nutrients, as well as an adequate humidity and temperature in their crops.

Quartz is one of the components of granite, which has the property of capturing solar energy, as well as to concentrate it and keep it, even after sunset. In that way, as the temperature maintains itself longer in the benched terraces, a good adaptation and domestication was propitiated for plants that came from warmer areas, such as coca, for example.

In Machupicchu, the agricultural benched terraces contain between 50 and 80 cm. of soil with humus.

On the lower Eastern side of Machupicchu's largest set of agricultural terraces, there are enclosures that were warehouses and homes **2**. These are the first enclosures that can be seen when entering to go on the tourist visit.

One of them might have been the home of one of the peasant families Bingham found there, upon his arrival, in 1911.

The Trail to Huaynapicchu **3**

Huayna Picchu means Young Mountain.

It was another very important Apu on the slopes of which one can appreciate benched terraces or contention walls and rooms that were left unfinished. In the excavations undertaken there, fine ceramics and metal adornments were found, which shows the ritual and ceremonial importance of that mountain.

On a daily basis, only 400 people are allowed to have access to it, with previous reservation.

It is a very steep trail that takes about 2 hours walking up and down. However, it is a rewarding route, with spectacular views of Machupicchu and its surrounding landscape.

It is the same path that goes up the Small Mountain or Huch'uypicchu, as well as to the Great Cave better known as the Temple of the Moon which is located on the lower back side of Mount Huaynapicchu, and requires much energy and more time to reach (About 3 hours to go its and come back).

The Path towards the Inkan Bridge

It is the shortest one, as it lasts about one hour to go and come back.

This simple bridge (Wooden beams stretched out to form a footbridge), ends up being an excellent technical solution, in that part of the trail.

It can perfectly well contain the effects of gravity, in the vertical cut in the mountain, and resist to loads it was submitted to.

The Path to Inti Punku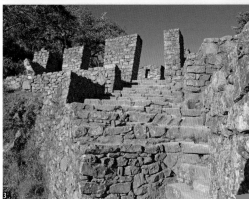

It is a hike that takes about 2 hours to go and come back.

The path in itself is an attraction, because of its quality and the presence of ceremonial places, which indicates its great importance, as it was the Main Trail or Inka Ñan, to access the city of Machupicchu.

Today, it fulfills the same function as it did in the past, for tourists who decide to hike the Inkan Trail which parts from Km. 82 or Km. 104 of the railway.

From Inti Punku, there are beautiful perspectives of Machupicchu.

View from Inti Punku ▼

Likewise, one can observe the Hiram Bingham Road that goes from Machupicchu Pueblo, better known to us as "Aguas Calientes", due to the presence of thermal springs at the entrance gate of the Inkan City of Machupicchu. This road was inaugurated in 1948, facilitating the arrival of millions of tourists.